D1453900

Buzzwords

Buzzwords

The Jargon of the 1990s

John Davis

Crown Trade Paperbacks
New York

To Jay Leno, master of American humor

Copyright © 1993 by John Davis

All rights reserved. No part of this book may be reproduced or transmitted in any form or by any means, electronic or mechanical, including photocopying, recording, or by any information storage and retrieval system, without permission in writing from the publisher.

Published by Crown Publishers, Inc., 201 East 50th Street, New York, New York 10022. Member of the Crown Publishing Group.
Random House, Inc. New York, Toronto, London, Sydney, Auckland.

CROWN Trade Paperbacks and colophon are trademarks of Crown Publishers, Inc.

Manufactured in the United States of America

Library of Congress Cataloging-in-Publication Data
Davis, John
    Buzzwords : the jargon of the 1990s / by John Davis. — 1st ed.
        p.   cm.
      1. English language—United States—Jargon—Dictionaries.
    2. United States—Popular culture—Dictionaries.   3. Americanisms—
    Dictionaries.   I. Title.
    PE1585.D38   1993
    427'.09—dc20
                                                                    93-19266
                                                                        CIP

ISBN 0-517-88060-1

10 9 8 7 6 5 4 3 2 1

First Edition

Introduction

In the spring of 1989, I chanced upon a hushed and hurried conversation between two emergency room physicians concerning the admission of an elderly bag lady who had been struck by a taxicab.

The doctors spoke English, not medical jargon, but I still didn't understand much of what they said. The next day, I tracked down one of them and, after much persuasion and promises of anonymity, I found out what he was talking about. Intrigued, I could not let the matter lie. I spent the better part of the past three years seeking out workers in all fields, all across the country, and extracting, under promises of *omerta,* their secret language. Thus was born *Buzzwords.*

"Buzzwords" are, in their essence, a subversive form of English. Unlike slang, which is meant to be overheard and to drift into general usage, buzzwords are intentionally the language of exclusion. Conversants, by sharing language only between themselves, exercise a unique form of verbal power.

What follows is a compendium of popular buzzwords, by profession. Virtually all of them have a sarcastic, humorous connotation. The reason is simple. Most workers treat the "good" or "normal" in their business without comment. It is the problems and difficult areas that tend to bring exasperation, stress, anger, and, eventually, the need for release.

When sufficiently provocative, life's challenges force people to react and, in reacting, to find and define a language that allows them to secretly complain, explain, retaliate, and commiserate. That reason alone was enough to make me want to put this book together. What made it even more enjoyable was the fact that most of the buzzwords are bizarre, strangely familiar, and incredibly funny.

This work would not have been possible without the assistance of dozens of talented, helpful people. Many of those who contributed much to this book insisted upon anonymity. While I respect and understand their decision, I thank them for their time, their advice, and their generous contributions. You know who you are and I salute you.

As for the rest, I owe a special thanks to the following: the staffs of the New York Public Library, the Boston Public Library, Carpenter Memorial Library, and the University of New Hampshire Library; Dr. James Borbotsina; Dr. Roger Fossum; Dr. John Wolf; Dr. Michael Mittelman; Michelle Houghton; Marc Metevier; Lieutenant Michael Clayton; Lisa Avery; William Ritchotte; John Clayton; Marc Shapiro; Tim Molan; Kay Gill; Pam Cross; Dan Healy; Ernie Van Tassel; Don Goulet; Linda Ramaska; Bob Connelley; Hope Hoag; David Murphy; Richard Marx; Roger Parmalee; Richard Lee; Ray Morrisette; Harvey De Vries; Jane Davis; Keith Moynihan; Steve Schubert; Carl Marshall; and Rita Davis.

Many thanks as well to Tracy Mailloux for the careful preparation and long hours spent typing this final manuscript and all of its drafts.

Buzzwords

Advertising Director

PUT THE PLAN IN THE CAN   Dumped the ad campaign

POPEYE   Point of purchase advertisement

GLOW BLOW   Testimonial

CANCER CURE   New product

RAGS 'N' MAGS   Newspapers and magazines

PICASSO   Art director

BAD ADS   Poorly designed display

METER CHEATER   Employee who inflates bills

NOSE HAIR   Client

e.g.—*"If that **METER CHEATER** keeps it up, that **NOSE HAIR**'s gonna get suspicious."*

DRIP DROPS   Residual payments

LIAR FOR HIRE   Ad copy writer

BRAIN SPRAIN   Concept

WINK 'N' DRINK   Trip for advertising executives

FLY BY   Sky write

BLUDGEON & TRUNCHEON (B&T)   Aggressive advertising to launch a new product

CLEAN KILL   Spot ad

MOBILE REPTILE   Traveling sales representative

SENILE REPTILE   Elderly sales representative

REJECTION DETECTION   Market research

e.g.—*"**PICASSO** wants to know if we have a **CLEAN KILL** for that **B&T** and how many **MOBILE REPTILES** are working on **REJECTION DETECTION**."*

BITCH OF A PITCH   Especially difficult sales presentation

BITCH PITCH   Sales presentation made by a female advertising representative

CLIP TRIP   Junket

THROW A BONE   Give away promotional products

DUPLICITY PUBLICITY   Completely false advertising claims

PRO CON   Publicist

e.g.—*"We better plan to **THROW SOME BONE** on that **CLIP TRIP**. I don't think the **PRO CON**'s gonna get them to fall for that **DUPLICITY PUBLICITY**."*

FULL NELSON   Hard sell

DISC JOCKEY (DJ)   Spin controller

GODZILLA   Client with a bad image

MOTHER TERESA   Client with a good image

e.g.—*"Even with the **FULL NELSON**, I think the **DJ**'s gonna have a tough time changing **GODZILLA** into **MOTHER TERESA**."*

CRONE ON THE PHONE   Persistent telemarketer

SCALE THE MAIL   Throw away mail without opening it

RAT   Consumer

e.g.—*"Those **RATS** keep **SCALING THE MAIL**. We better get a **CRONE ON THE PHONE** soon."*

SLOPPY COPY   Poorly worded press release

BRIDGE JUMPER   Stunt

e.g.—*"Who wrote the **SLOPPY COPY** for that **BRIDGE JUMPER**?"*

FEE SPREE   Excessive billing

HICKEY   Favorable review

CHEAP STAKE   Lottery contest with an inexpensive giveaway; a.k.a. CHEAP-SKATE SWEEPSTAKE

SNEAK ATTACK   Subliminal advertising

CHECK WITH CHUCK   Market survey; a.k.a. CALL SAUL

DISOWN THE PHONE   Abruptly end a telemarketing campaign

GOEBBELS   Head of public relations

PEN HEADS   Print media

STRANGLE   Stop an unfavorable news story

e.g.—*"GOEBBELS says to DISOWN THE PHONE right away. While you're at it, see if you can get one of those PEN HEADS to STRANGLE that story."*

FLASH 'N' DASH   Photo opportunity
BRIDE BOX   Media kit
KNOT   Product tie-in; a.k.a. CHAIN
PUSH THE TUSH   Publicity tour
SAVE THE QUEEN   Crisis management
PUB IT 'N' RUB IT CLUB   Public affairs department
LAB RATS   Focus group
CLUSTER BOMB   Multimedia advertising campaign
DENT   Product impact

e.g.—*"How many DENTS did they count when they CLUSTER BOMBED those LAB RATS?"*

OUT SHOUT   Voice-over
JINGLE ON A SHINGLE   Scrap a musical refrain
THROAT GRABBER   Using children in soft-sell advertising

e.g.—*"First of all, we needed an OUT SHOUT. But the music's so bad, we put the JINGLE ON A SHINGLE. Maybe we should try a THROAT GRABBER instead."*

SHOOT THE FRUIT   Make a commercial for a psychiatric hospital
FLAIL THE MAIL   Aggressively pursue mailing list names

Beauty Contest Director

NO-BRAIN TRAIN   Rehearsal
GANGPLANK   Runway
HAGSTER   Former beauty queen

e.g.—*"Okay, you can get those HAGSTERS out on the GANGPLANK. It's NO-BRAIN TRAIN time."*

QUAYLE CARDS   Q (cue) cards; a.k.a. IDIOT CARDS

STALIN   Contest director
BRAILLE BOARD   TelePrompTer

e.g.—*"STALIN wants the QUAYLE CARDS and BRAILLE BOARD set up now!"*

FROSTING   Makeup; a.k.a. PAINT
KENNEL KLUB   Rival contestants
SLIP GRIP   Wardrobe
HONKER HELPER   Silicon implants
NO CLOTHES POSE   Nude photo session
CHOP 'N' CHANNEL   Plastic surgery

e.g.—*"Linda said she definitely needed HONKER HELPERS for the NO CLOTHES POSE; personally I think she's been CHOPPED 'N' CHANNELED more than once."*

THREW THE SHREW   Evicted a stage mother
CLAMMY PAMMY   Sick contestant
BUSH PUSH   Get endorsements; a.k.a. HUSTLE THE BUSTLE
FACE RACE   Beauty contest
TIT TIP   Gifts
FLASH THE FLESH   Win the bathing suit competition
GRAB 'N' GROPE   Sexual harassment
LEECHES   Judges
MUTE THE FLUTE   Bad musical performance
SHABBY ABBY   Poorly outfitted contestant
BEST CHEST   Big breasted; a.k.a. LOCKERS FOR KNOCKERS
HOOTER COMPUTER   Measurements
BROAD MAUDE   Contestant with large hips

e.g.—*"The LEECHES want SHABBY ABBY checked on the HOOTER COMPUTER. She doesn't look like she's got the BEST CHEST. Who's the BROAD MAUDE?"*

WAVIN MAVEN   Enthusiastic contestant in a motorcade or parade
SPEECH TEACH   Public speaking or elocution lesson
LEAP TO SLEEP   Dramatic reading
NOISE BOYZ   Stage band

FULL MOON   Large buttocks; a.k.a. TONS O' BUNS
RIPPLES FOR NIPPLES   No chest; a.k.a. QUEST FOR A CHEST

e.g.—*"Look at it this way, she may have **RIPPLES FOR NIPPLES** but she's got **TONS O' BUNS**."*

BLURT SPURT   Media interviews
RANDY FOR SANDY   Sexual proposition
MISSING CEREBRAL CORTEX (MCC)   Master of ceremonies
HORSE SPRAY   Bouquet
CLAP CAP   Crown
TRASH CLASH   Evening gown competition
SEALS   Audience members
LOW-DOWN SHOWDOWN   Talent contest
GLASS BREAKER   Opera singer
FLUTE TOOT   Musical instrument player
TRIPPER   Dancer
PAY FOR PLAY   Scholarship
VALLEY   Cleavage
CURTAIN CRETINS   Stage hands

e.g.—*"Go check and see what those **CURTAIN CRETINS** have done with the podium. Did you notice the big **VALLEY** on Ms. Idaho?"*

OBESE CLARISSE   Fat contestant
EXTRA LARGE MARGE   Very fat contestant
SCRAWNY BONNIE   Emaciated contestant

e.g.—*"Put **OBESE CLARISSE** and **EXTRA LARGE MARGE** in the last row. **SCRAWNY BONNIE** goes up front."*

FUMBLE 'N' STUMBLE   Answer questions poorly
CLASS ASS   Shapely buttocks
TITS WON'T QUIT   Well-proportioned bust

e.g.—*"Those **SEALS** went wild at the **TRASH CLASH**. Wait'll they catch the **LOW-DOWN SHOWDOWN**."*

Car Dealer

BIG LIE TECHNIQUE   Sales pitch
MADAM CURIE   Mercury
NEW BILL   Consumer who's willing to pay more than the sticker price
COOLER   Air conditioning
PUKE SHOW   Peugeot

e.g.—*"The NEW BILL wants to know whether that PUKE SHOW comes with a COOLER."*

PANZER   Mercedes-Benz
ABUSED   Used
DICKER ON THE STICKER   Negotiate
FOLDMOBILE   Oldsmobile
SLATTERN   Saturn
SNOOZE PATROL   Cruise control
SMOG LOG   Emissions test
ZOO KEY   Suzuki
PURSE   Female prospect
BEAGLE   Eagle
CHEEP   Jeep
DAMP STAMP   Forged safety sticker
CAR BAR   Sales lot
JAP TRAP   Toyota

e.g.—*"Make sure that JAP TRAP has a DAMP STAMP before you put it out in the CAR BAR."*

VOLCANO   Car that burns a lot of oil
DODGEM   Dodge; a.k.a. DODGIT or DODGER
STEALER   Dealer
CARDIAC   Cadillac
BUSTED   Accident damage
STAB   Saab; a.k.a. SLAB
BIG THIGHS   Midsize

STIFF PRICK Stick shift
MONDO BONDO Used a lot of body filler
PORCH Porsche
BLOT ROT Rust
YELL BELL Theft alarm
REGURGITATE Rebate; a.k.a. SPIT-UP
BORED Ford
FUTILITY Utility vehicle
BENT QUARTER Trade-in
WAIF Inexperienced buyer
CROAKWAGON Volkswagen
REAL ROUGH Cream puff
CRUTCH Clutch
ASS Chassis

e.g.—*"Tell the* **WAIF** *I'm not interested in his* **BENT QUARTER**. *That* **CROAKWAGON**'s **REAL ROUGH**. *It needs some* **ASS** *work and a new* **CRUTCH**."

WITHOUT SHOTS Without a warranty
LOSING CHANGE Cruising range
I'LL SUE YOU Isuzu
CRY SIR Chrysler
PUNT IT BACK Pontiac
BLEW IT Buick
HEAVY CHEVY Full-size Chevrolet
MPG Miles per gram of gas
PUMP THE CHUMP Push an option package
SNICKER PRICE Sticker price; a.k.a. STICK 'EM PRICE
NAZI LAND CRUISER (NLC) German car
GOOK COUPE Japanese car

e.g.—*"It's getting harder and harder to sell any* **CARDIACS** *nowadays. Everybody wants an* **NLC** *or a* **GOOK COUPE**."

TAKE SOME LAPS Road test
DIDN'T INHALE PRICE (DIP) Sales price
POOR BOY Buyer; a.k.a. FISH IN A BARREL (FIB)

e.g.—*"***POOR BOY** *wants to know the* **DIP** *before he* **TAKES SOME LAPS**."

LUNCH MONEY   Down payment
BUY 'N' DIE   Hyundai
SLOPE SLED   Nissan
DEATH PENALTY   Lemon-law violation
DARTH NADER   Ralph Nader
FACELIFT   Rolling back the odometer

e.g.—*"Thanks to **DARTH NADER**, you get the **DEATH PENALTY** if you get caught doing a **FACELIFT**."*

SLEAZEMAN   Salesman
TRUST PROOF   Rustproof
WANDA   Honda
U WON'T   Yugo
SHRINK WRAPPED   Crash tested

e.g.—*"What happened when they **SHRINK WRAPPED** that **BEAGLE**?"*

FOOL INSPECTION   Fuel injection
SEEDY PLAYER   CD player

Coroner

ORGAN GRINDER   Coroner
PIGEON   Foul play
PUNCHING BAG   Trauma victim
TICKET   Toe tag; a.k.a. LICENSE
SLIT 'N' SPLIT   Make an incision
ENGINE   Brain
WIDE RECEIVER   Bludgeon victim; a.k.a. DENT
VEGGIE BIN   Refrigerated storage
MITTENS   Rubber gloves
JOYSTICK   Scalpel

e.g.—*"Before we get that **DENT** outta the **VEGGIE BIN**, I've gotta find my **MITTENS** and **JOYSTICK**."*

DETERMINATION FOR THE EXTERMINATION   Decision on the cause of death; a.k.a. FIVE-DAY FORECAST

CONDOM   Rubber body bag

COUGH DROP   Smoke inhalation victim

e.g.—*"Who made the FIVE-DAY FORECAST on that COUGH DROP in the CONDOM?"*

REJECTIVES   Detectives; a.k.a. DEFECTIVES

ORGANIC   Dead by natural causes

LUNCH BUCKET   Stomach contents

ZINC DRINK   Death by poison

e.g.—*"The REJECTIVES want us to check out this guy's LUNCH BUCKET. They don't think he's ORGANIC. They think someone slipped him a ZINC DRINK."*

CHUCKLES   Undertaker; a.k.a. GIGGLES

PLAY-DOH   Viscera

COOKIE SHEET   Examining table

e.g.—*"I'm all done with this Play-Doh. Help GIGGLES get the WIDE RECEIVER off the COOKIE SHEET."*

CORED IN HIS FORD   Died in a traffic accident; a.k.a. FOUND HIS CHEVY IN THE LEVEE

CLEAN THE FRIDGE   Take a body out of the compartment

CHAINSAW   Cranial saw

OODLES OF NOODLES   Severe brain injury with leakage; a.k.a. GRAVY DRAIN

BLOTTER   Trauma victim

TURKEY   Stabbing victim

STOP THE MAIL   Time of death

BOUGHT A SHOT   Gunshot victim

PORTHOLES   Bullet wounds

OPEN HOUSE   Autopsy

YO-YO   Suicide by hanging

M&M   Mass-murder victim

FLIP A COIN   Determine sex of victim

e.g.—*"After the **OPEN HOUSE** on that **YO-YO**, call the **DEFECTIVES**. They want you to help **FLIP A COIN** on an old **M&M**."*

SLING RING   Ligature mark
DESPISE DEMISE   Crime of passion
BODY POTTY   Coroner's office
NO RIDER   Coroner's van
CHEESECAKE   Decomposing body; a.k.a. CRUMBLER

e.g.—*"We need a **NO RIDER** to take that **CHEESECAKE** to the **BODY POTTY**."*

TRAIN TRACKS   Sutures
START YOUR ENGINE   Begin Y-shaped incision
SINKHOLE   Cranial cavity
GOODIES   Vital organs
TAXICAB   Toxicology lab

e.g.—*"After you **START YOUR ENGINE**, send the **GOODIES** to the **TAXICAB**. I'll put **TRAIN TRACKS** in the **SINKHOLE**."*

TOP CHOP   Chief forensic pathologist
TICKER FLICKER   Heart attack
POX TROT   Bacterial infection
SLIDE SHOW   Coroner's inquest
DROP A BAG ON THE HAG   Mercy killing

e.g.—*"According to the **SLIDE SHOW**, Fenwick didn't **DROP A BAG ON THE HAG**. She had a **TICKER FLICKER**."*

THOMAS NO GUCCIS   Dr. Thomas Noguchi
ANVIL   Drowning victim
GAS CAN   Fire victim

e.g.—*"That **ORGAN GRINDER** may not be **THOMAS NO GUCCIS**, but he ought to be able to tell the difference between an **ANVIL** and a **GAS CAN**."*

TUX   Lab coat
FUSE   Electrocution victim
COCK LOCK   Venereal disease
LUNG SPRUNG   Death by suffocation

FROG IN HIS THROAT   Death by choking
DECEASE RELEASE   Turn over the body to next of kin
EXPIRATION DATE   Time of death
CROAK ON THE SMOKE   Die of lung cancer
TAGGED BY A CEMENT BAG   Killed in a construction site

Cruise Ship Director

CHAIR FARE   Seating capacity
SCROUNGE   Lounge
BRANDY ANDY   Wine steward
BOVINE ROOM   Dining room
HEIFERS   Obese passengers
DISH FISH   Dining stewards
EMBEZZLER   Purser
CIGAR BOX   Safe

e.g.—*"Here, give this necklace to the **EMBEZZLER** and tell him to put it in the **CIGAR BOX**."*

WHITE BLIGHT   Crew
BUMP 'N' JUMP   Evacuation drill; a.k.a. SCREAM 'N' CRY
STUCK IN THE MUCK   Run aground

e.g.—*"Even without those **HEIFERS**, we still got **STUCK IN THE MUCK** last week."*

SHAM SLAM   Duty-free shop
LEMMINGS   Passengers
LIFELESS   Life vest or jacket
CORNHOLED THE HOLD   Hit an iceberg
FLY-BY-NIGHT CLUB   Night club
SONG KILLERS   Lounge act

e.g.—*"There'll be a mutiny on board if we don't get those **SONG KILLERS** outta the **FLY-BY-NIGHT CLUB**."*

PIERRE   Concierge

DREKFEST Breakfast
CARDIAC ATTRACT Jogging track
LOSER CRUISER Singles cruise
CLUB DEAD Club Med
PUSBOY Busboy
CANCER ENHANCER Passenger with a dark tan
BLIGH Captain
BLIGH'S THIGH Captain's table
BOD SQUAD Pool attendants
TUNA LAGUNA Swimming pool

e.g.—*"CANCER ENHANCER says one of the filters broke. Better get the BOD SQUAD over to the TUNA LAGUNA."*

SURVIVAL Arrival
PLANKTON Bottom-deck passenger
POSTCARD Coast Guard
SHARK FISHING Fell overboard

e.g.—*"Time for the POSTCARD. That PLANKTON just went SHARK FISHING."*

TUNA CAN Cabin; a.k.a. SMALL HALL
TUNA HELPER Cabin attendant
STUPID Steward
SHEEP DIP Hors d'oeuvres
FLATTENED THE FERRY Hit another boat
VIKING FUNERAL Fire

e.g.—*"Uh-oh, we just FLATTENED THAT FERRY. Hope we're not in for a VIKING FUNERAL."*

GREEN TEAM Seasick
BEAN Day tourist
REFRIED BEAN Drunken day tourist
FLASHLIGHT Lighthouse
PUT ON CLEAN SOCKS Dress for dinner
HOLE IN THE BOWL Spring a leak
TIME FOR SWIMMING LESSONS Abandon ship

e.g.—"BLIGH says we have a HOLE IN THE BOWL. TIME FOR SWIMMING LESSONS."

FALL IN THE HALL   Rough seas
WALK 'N' GAWK   Sightsee
GLOOM SERVANTS   Room service
DEAF CHEF   A chef who screwed up the food order
ALBANIAN JUGGLERS   Theater show
CHEESE 'N' CRACKERS   Captain's welcoming party

e.g.—"STUPID told me the ALBANIAN JUGGLERS will be on after the CHEESE 'N' CRACKERS."

HUMP THE GROOMER   Honeymooner
SPOT THE SANDBAR   Sight land
FOLLOW THE OIL SLICK   Chart a course
DROP THE BODY   Set anchor
BEAT THE SHEETS   Change the bed furnishings and linens
BIG DOG   Top-deck passenger
BUTT SLING   Deck chair
LOUD CROWD   Noisy night club
GOLDEN GATE   Bridge

e.g.—"We've got a LOUD CROWD tonight. One of the LEMMINGS was so drunk he threw a BUTT SLING off the GOLDEN GATE."

SHOVEL IT OVERBOARD   Shuffleboard
BREAD LINE   Buffet lunch
WALRUS   Waiter

Dating Service Manager

CHIP TRIP   Computer date
DEBENTURE   "Financially secure"
MIRROR-BREAKING   "Average looking"
BOY PLOY   Woman's personal ad
KLAXON   "Conversationalist"; a.k.a. EARPLUG

UNINHABITED "Uninhibited"

ANOREXIC "Slim"

EAR-SUCKING "Romantic"

HAMSTER-DIDDLING "Animal lover"

SHARECROPPER "Nature freak"; a.k.a. BUNYAN

e.g.—*"Basically, she's an **ANOREXIC, UNINHABITED KLAXON**, hoping to find an **EAR-SUCKING, HAMSTER-DIDDLING SHARECROPPER**."*

HELEN KELLER Blind date

DWARF "Petite"

TABLE-HOPPING "Extroverted"

ROTO-ROOTING "Adventurous"

QUIZ CAM Video date

TUXEDO Marriage potential

ALCOHOLIC "Social drinker"

JUNIOR COLLEGE "Educated"; a.k.a. EIGHTH GRADER, VOC TECH

BELLHOP "Executive"

BLACK HAT Widow

TOE-KISSING "Submissive"

PILE DRIVER "Stud"

GORILLA "Full-figured"

DRIP TRIP Singles cruise

SEMI-FEMI "Bisexual"

HIGH-HEELED "Dominant"; a.k.a. BIG BOOT

e.g.—*"That **BLACK HAT** wants to meet a **TOE-KISSING PILE DRIVER**. Who's the **HIGH-HEELED SEMI-FEMI GORILLA** I saw on the **DRIP TRIP?**"*

BROW BEAT Interview

LOST CAUSE Single parent

CASTRATER "Feminist"

HANDS OFF "Sensitive"

DOG "Attractive"

FART-HOLDING "Cultured"

CHIMNEY "Smoker"; a.k.a. BLACK LUNGER

VACUUMED Divorced

TRUFFLE SHUFFLE Dinner dance

DREDGE UP SOMETHING   Meet someone
BAD COOK   Widower
BAIT BOX   Dating service

e.g.—*"Maybe we can interest that **BAD COOK** in the **BAIT BOX**. Who knows, he might **DREDGE UP SOMETHING** at the **TRUFFLE SHUFFLE**."*

ENSLAVED   Engaged
KICKING TIRES   Dating
NOSE RING   "Offbeat"
DAHMER   "Slightly neurotic"
COUCH TRIP   One-night stand
MR. WRONG   "Ladies' man"
FUEL INJECTED   "Light drinker"
MUSCLE HOUND   "Weight lifter"
MOIST   "Passionate"

e.g.—*"She told me that **MR. WRONG** was a **COUCH TRIP**. No more **FUEL INJECTED MUSCLE HOUNDS** for her. Maybe we can fix her up with that **MOIST CHIMNEY**."*

CRUNCH LUNCH   Break a dinner date
ZIPPER FLIPPER   Flirt
TROTTER   "Good looking"
POTLUCK PARADE   Singles bar
BIGAMIST   "Single"
FEEDBAG   Feedback
DESPERATE   "Sincere"
PSYCHOTIC   "Warm"
HYDRANT   Chaperon; a.k.a. DEAD WEIGHT
HEMLOCK HAMHOCK   Supper dance
AIDS CANDIDATE   "Swinger"
HEAD-ON CRASH   Perfect match
CARPET   "Agreeable"
HAREBRAINED   "Spontaneous"
EUNUCH   "Opera lover"
PREVIOUSLY DIAGNOSED   "Clean"

e.g.—*"Well, we've got at least one **HEAD-ON CRASH**. A **PREVIOUSLY***

DIAGNOSED, HAREBRAINED AIDS CANDIDATE met a CARPET EUNUCH."

MEGAPHONE   "Soft-spoken"
STOCK OFFERING   Fee
SPENDTHRIFT   Client
BOOKING SHEET   Interview or intake chart
LEMON LIST   Dating directory

Day-Care Operator

GET HORIZONTAL   Naptime
SING SING   Playpen
LOADED GUN   Crayon
PROTECTIVE CUSTODY (PC)   In the corner
BUMPY   Child with mumps
SHED   Quarantine
BOMBER PILOT   Toilet trained
BARRACUDA   Big eater

e.g.—"*Get that* **LOADED GUN** *away from Tim and put him in* **PC**. *Is that* **BARRACUDA** *a* **BOMBER PILOT** *or not?*"

CURSES 'N' CRIMES   Nursery rhymes
FLAME GAME   Fire drill
WIDGETS   Preschoolers
BAIL OUT   Get dropped off
WARDEN   Supervisor
BORING BOOK   Story book
HOTHEAD   Feverish child
SNATCHED   Picked up
RAINCOAT   Bib
STEAM SHOVEL   Spoon feed
REJECTED   Vomited
CATAPULT   Seesaw
TOXIC CLEANUP   Diaper changing

CREEPING CRUD   Diaper rash
STEAK KNIFE   Pacifier
SIDEWINDER   Sleeping child
SKYBOX   High chair
HURL WHIRL   Merry-go-round
QUEASY EASY   Repeat bouts of nausea
LIFEBOAT   Blanket
FUSS BUS   Cranky child

e.g.—*"The FUSS BUS in the SKYBOX wants his STEAK KNIFE."*

CEREAL KILLER   Picky eater
COOL GRUEL   Cold breakfast

e.g.—*"I'd be a CEREAL KILLER too if I had to eat that COOL GRUEL."*

QUIZ LIZ   Telephone inquiry
SMACK ATTACK   Use excessive corporal punishment
RANSOM   Weekly charges
WARM BUNS   Spank

e.g.—*"I've got a QUIZ LIZ on the line. She wants to know if we WARM BUNS and how much the RANSOM is."*

UNCLE LOUIE   Child abuser
BIG HOUSE   Day-care center
DROP 'N' SWAP   Change of clothes
MEDDLERS   Parents
AMBUSH   Unscheduled visit
DESTRUCTOR   Instructor
DIDDLE WITH HER FIDDLE   Sexually molest a young girl
BLISTER HIS SISTER   Fight between siblings; a.k.a. SMOTHER HER
    BROTHER
LAVA CHUNKS   Hot lunch
NEEDS A HOSE FOR HIS NOSE   Child with a bad head cold
ESCAPEE   Child who leaves the grounds
REDHEAD   Child with measles

e.g.—*"REDHEAD's gotta go into the SHED until he gets SNATCHED. Tommy definitely NEEDS A HOSE FOR HIS NOSE. While you're at it, tell Matt he can't BLISTER HIS SISTER anymore."*

BOOT CAMP   Kindergarten

DIPSTICK   Oral thermometer

BULLPEN   Playground

SAHARA   Sandbox

DEATHGRIP   Stuffed animal

DRUNKEN SAILOR   Child learning to walk

BREAK GLASSES   Sing songs

CAGE   Lunchroom

SCREAMER   Infant

e.g.—*"The **MEDDLER** wants to know if we would take both **DRUNKEN SAILORS** and **SCREAMERS**."*

CATTLE DRIVE   Prepare the children to leave

TERRORIZE THE LITTLE GUYS   Read scary stories

LAUNCH CONTROL   Swings

KICK THE KITTENS   Retrieve boots and mittens

BILGE PUFFS   Snacks

TRAMPLE LENA   Trampoline

e.g.—*"First, **TRAMPLE LENA** time. Then they can have their **BILGE PUFFS**."*

Dentist

NAPKIN   Lead apron

CHERNOBYL   X-ray area

GRAB SOME CHANGE   Extract a tooth

BACK POCKET   Rear teeth, particularly the wisdom teeth

e.g.—*"Hey, Marge! Get Mrs. Johnson a **NAPKIN** and send her to **CHERNOBYL** while I **GRAB SOME CHANGE** out of Tim's **BACK POCKET**!"*

CATTLE   Patients; a.k.a. SHEEP

STOCKYARD   Reception area

DALE EVANS   Receptionist

e.g.—*"Things are really backing up around here. Tell **DALE EVANS** to drive some **CATTLE** out of the **STOCKYARD** or we'll be here all night!"*

SQUIRT THE DIRT   Bleach teeth
SLIT 'N' SPIT   Gum surgery
AUDIT   Semiannual dental checkup
SINGLE   Small cavity
TRIPLE   Big cavity
SHUT OUT   No cavities
HOME RUN   Periodontal disease
WALLET   Dental insurance; a.k.a. the TOOTH FAIRY

e.g.—*"I thought the Hoffman twins were gonna get **SHUT OUT**. Luckily, Amy had two **TRIPLES** and a **SINGLE**, and Amanda just hit a **HOME RUN**. Check with their mother and make sure she's got her **WALLET**."*

CHILL PILL   Novocain injection
SUCK 'N' CHUCK   Clean out a diseased tooth
DROOL STOOL   Dental chair; a.k.a. GROAN THRONE, BLEAT SEAT

e.g.—*"After you get her in the **DROOL STOOL**, give her a **CHILL PILL** and then we can **SUCK 'N' CHUCK** it."*

CRAMMED 'N' JAMMED   Impacted wisdom tooth
GRAPPLING HOOK   Forceps
RAW JAW   Sore mouth
TOXIC   Bad breath
GUMMO   Patient missing many teeth
SCREW   Dental implant
DRUDGE   Hygienist
LEONA   An especially vocal, complaining, unsympathetic patient
SUPER NO-LEAD   Nitrous oxide
TORTURE CHAMBER   Examination room
GRATING   Whining, crying behavior

e.g.—*"Have a **DRUDGE** drag **LEONA** into the **TORTURE CHAMBER**. If she keeps **GRATING**, fill her up with **SUPER NO-LEAD**."*

SIREN   Screaming child
MACHINE GUN   Dental drill

BRAIN KILLER   Silver filling
RESERVED SEAT   Gold tooth; a.k.a. FRONT ROW.
GRENADE   Lollipop

e.g.—*"This **SIREN**'s all done with his **AUDIT**. While I grab a **MACHINE GUN**, ask the mother whether she wants a **BRAIN KILLER** or **RESERVED SEAT**. And make sure the kid gets a **GRENADE** when he leaves."*

CANAL PAL   Periodontist
SCUM IN THE GUM   Deep pocket of disease
SEWER   Badly abscessed tooth
HOWLER   Emergency patient
DR. MENGELE   Oral surgeon

e.g.—*"That **HOWLER**'s **SEWER** is awful big. We may have to send him to **DR. MENGELE**."*

PROSPECTING   Root canal therapy
FULL HOUSE   Lots of rotten teeth
SILVER BULLET   Toothbrush
BROOKLYN   Bridge
SEDATE RAPE   Fondling a patient after sedation
RED RIVER   Bleeding gums
CAPTAIN HOOK   Orthodontist
CHOP THE TOP   Correct an overbite
METAL MOUTH   Patient with braces

e.g.—*"She'll be a **METAL MOUTH** after **CAPTAIN HOOK CHOPS THE TOP**."*

MARILYN QUAYLE   Patient with buck teeth
PIANO TUNE   Fix misaligned teeth
ROLEX   Braces; a.k.a. HEAVY METAL, ANGLE IRONS

e.g.—*"**MARILYN QUAYLE**'s gonna have to have her **PIANO TUNED** pronto. Lemme know what size **ROLEX** I'll need."*

NUTRASIZING   Transmitting AIDS

e.g.—*"Make sure to wear your mask and keep a close eye on Fenwick. I don't want him **NUTRASIZING** us accidentally."*

GOOF IN THE ROOF   Cleft palate
ROOT BRUTE   Endodontist
SPITTOON   Sterilization tray
PAIN CRANE   Dental probe
BUM GUM   Gum disease
RIPPED HIS LIP   Dental malpractice

Dermatologist

PIGEON SHIT   Port wine stain
LIGHT SHOW   Laser surgery; a.k.a. LIGHT SHOWER

e.g.—*"It's time to get **PIGEON SHIT** in here for the **LIGHT SHOW**."*

FOREST   Patient with excess body hair
FIN ON THE SKIN   Wart
BROWN BAG   Mole
SICK SACK   Cyst
SNIP 'N' CLIP   Excise
RASPUTIN   Patient with a lot of facial hair
OIL SPILL   Pimples
CRATER   Acne

e.g.—*"If you look closely at **RASPUTIN**, you'll see an **OIL SPILL** and a **SICK SACK**."*

RED MAN   Patient with sunburn
GUNK   Cream
FULL DECK   Room full of patients
BAD ROAD   Mumps
POLKA DOTS   Measles
LEOPARD   Liver spots
WHITE BREAD   Albino
GASPIN' IN ASPEN   Rocky Mountain spotted fever
FREEZER BURN   Frostbite
CAUGHT THE ROT   Developed gangrene
GRAVY   Pus

TIC TOC   Lyme disease

e.g.—*"It's not just FREEZER BURN. Smith has definitely CAUGHT THE ROT."*

BAG   Blister
DICK SICK   Genital warts
WATER BUCKET   Edema
TRIPLE CHIN   Goiter
DIVOT   Ulcer
MAKE THE GERM SQUIRM   Apply an antibacterial agent
DRAPE 'N' SCRAPE   Dermabrasion

e.g.—*"The DIVOT's too big to DRAPE 'N' SCRAPE. We better MAKE THE GERM SQUIRM."*

DIP 'N' SIP   Perform a biopsy
AROMA OF MELANOMA   Symptom of skin cancer

e.g.—*"I detect the AROMA OF MELANOMA. We better DIP 'N' SIP it."*

CHINESE TAN   Jaundice
MELLOW YELLOW   Impetigo
RICE   Lice
BASH THE RASH   Fungicide
SHOT SHOCK   Allergic reaction to medication
WINTERIZE   Freeze
PAW POX   Plantar warts
SOCK DOC   Dermatologist specializing in foot diseases
CANCER MAGNET   Baby oil

e.g.—*"WHITE BREAD is gonna be a RED MAN if he keeps using that CANCER MAGNET."*

DRIP ON THE LIP   Cold sore
TOE JAM   Athlete's foot
CROTCH CRUD   Venereal disease
BAKING A CAKE   Yeast infection
FLAKER   Patient with psoriasis

e.g.—*"We're almost done. All we've got left is a FLAKER. I thought Sally had CROTCH CRUD at first but she was only BAKING A CAKE."*

CANCER COAT   Tanning lotion
CAKE   Scab
FESTER ON CHESTER   Herpes
LOUSE IN THE MOUTH   Thrush
GERM WORM   Parasitic bacterial skin infection
STUFFED CABBAGE   Swollen tissue
SCABIES HAD BABIES   Rash is spreading
ROOSTER BOOSTER   Chicken pox shot
PRICKLED PICKLE   Jock itch

Disc Jockey

ASS-UP   "A" side
PERFECT DICKHEAD (PD)   Program director
SLUSH MUSH   Soft rock
DISASTER TAPE   Master tape
PURSE SNATCHER   Personal manager; a.k.a. PERSONAL DISASTER
FLICK THE STIX   Dub
SOCKER ROCKER   Sound engineer
HEADSTONE   Headphones
SEDUCER   Producer
COKE 'N' COLA   Payola
RHYME TIME   Air time

e.g.—*"That SEDUCER better drop some COKE 'N' COLA over here or he's not gonna get any RHYME TIME."*

SPACE STATION   Radio station
DENOUNCER   Announcer
FART CLUSTER   Chart buster
CLAP 'N' FLAP   Gospel song
CRUMMY DUMMY   Poor demonstration tape
SWIMMING IN SHOES   Rhythm and blues
PRONE TO BE CLONED   Recording likely to be bootlegged
ROOM KEY   Groupie
FUR LURE   Tour

BLUE TATTOOS   Punk-rock group

FARTIST   Artist

DOZER   Classical music

MOP-TOP BOP   Reggae

JOKE ROCK   Folk rock

COAL   Soul

DOORMAT   Format

BLEW GAS   Bluegrass

TRASHVILLE   Nashville

e.g.—*"When's that **BLEW GAS** festival in **TRASHVILLE?"***

CORPUS DELICTI   CD

ACCOMPLICE   Accompanist

BAND BRAND   Label

STINGER   Single; a.k.a. TINGLE

BIGGEST TITS   Greatest hits

VERY MENTAL   Heavy metal

ROCKER LOCKER   Record library

e.g.—*"Go down to the **ROCKER LOCKER** and see if you can find that **BIGGEST TITS** album for that **VERY MENTAL** group."*

BAWLING 'N' FALLING   Live concert

SUCKER PUCKER   Lip sync

HOOTER TOOTERS   Female band

COMA TUNES   Easy listening

LURCH IN CHURCH   Religious music

FLACK TRACK   Recording studio

SIX-GUN CITY   Motown

DUMB JACKASS   Disc jockey

BALL 'N' CHAIN   Contract

DROP   Release a record

SPRAWL 'N' CRAWL   Hip-hop

FOUL MOUTH   FM radio

COLD 'N' MOLDY   Golden oldie

SALAD   Ballad

PUKE BOX   Jukebox

HUNGRY 'N' DESPERATE   Country and western

SOP MUSIC   Pop music

e.g.—*"Go check out that **PUKE BOX**. All I saw in there were **HUNGRY 'N'
DESPERATE SALADS** and **SOP MUSIC**."*

ROCKMAN   Walkman
LUMP   Headbanger
ROCKIN ROBBY   Tape pirate
DEADWHANGER   Headbanger
STARE TIME   Air time

e.g.—*"How much more **STARE TIME** do we have to give to those
DEADWHANGERS?"*

CHAIR   Cher
U BLEW   U2
MENTALLICA   Metallica
DRUGS UP NOSES   Guns N' Roses
LACK TOES   Black Crowes
SHITHEAD O'CONNOR   Sinead O'Connor
2 DEAD SHREWS   2 Live Crew

Drug Counselor

BUSTED 'N' DUSTED   Arrested and photographed
TOMB   Drug treatment center
RUSH FLUSH   Detoxification
CONNED THE BOND   Made bail
U-TURN   Diversion program
RETAILER   Drug dealer
LONG JOHNS   Police
CRYIN TIME   Long jail sentence

e.g.—*"I hear the **LONG JOHNS** got that **RETAILER** over on Second Street.
He better hope that he pulls a **U-TURN** or he's in for some **CRYIN TIME**."*

DOPE POPE   Drug lord
FAIR-WEATHER FRIENDS   Colombian drug dealers

COOK 'N' HOOK Lab for manufacturing drugs

DOPE DICKS Narcotics detectives

WAKIN 'N' SHAKIN Stop taking drugs cold turkey

STONE ZONE Addict's home

FLIP TRIP Drug-induced hallucination

STIFF SNIFF Drug addict

e.g.—*"When we got the STIFF SNIFF out of the STONE ZONE, he was on a FLIP TRIP. He's been WAKIN 'N' SHAKIN since we first got him in the TOMB."*

STOOP 'N' SNOOP Drug raid; a.k.a. GRAB THE LAB, LIGHTS OUT

CHATTER CLATTER Informer

JITTERBUG Delirium tremens

BREAK THE SHAKE Gradual alcohol withdrawal

AMBASSADOR Drug courier

X-RAY Profile

STOP 'N' SHOP Customs inspection

e.g.—*"Since the AMBASSADOR fit the X-RAY, he was STOPPED 'N' SHOPPED at the border."*

MAIN COURSE Over-the-counter drugs

ELMER One who inhales chemicals by sticking head in a bag; a.k.a. BAG BRAIN

WILTIN MILTON Drug addict in withdrawal; a.k.a. SHRINKIN LINCOLN

ROOM AT THE TOMB Vacancy in a drug treatment center

GLIDE 'N' SLIDE Attempts to evade court-ordered supervision

CON JOHN Probation officer

DIGGING FOR GOLD Urine testing

e.g.—*"No more GLIDE 'N' SLIDE for that BAG BRAIN. CON JOHN's been DIGGING FOR GOLD."*

FULL HOUSE Family therapy

WALLBANGER Withdrawal symptoms

RIPE PIPE Drug supply

e.g.—*"Wilson's been WALLBANGING ever since he got BUSTED 'N' DUSTED. The DOPE DICKS are still looking for his RETAILER's RIPE PIPE."*

BUY 'N' FLY   Purchase drugs
PILL THRILL   Prescription addiction
BACK ON CRACK   High on drugs again
DOPE COPE   Counseling
RADAR   Electronic monitoring by means of an ankle cuff
DOPEC   Drug cartel

e.g.—*"DOPEC's been out of business since two major **RETAILERS** got **BUSTED 'N' DUSTED** last month."*

SOURCE OF THE HORSE   Synthetic heroin lab
TOOT SHOOT   Syringe
DRUG JUGS   Paraphernalia
CEMENT HEAD   Glue sniffer
BOTTLE BABY   Alcoholic
BACKBOARD   Miss the point of injection
BEAT A DEAD HORSE   Try to counsel a heroin addict
SICK VIC   Drinker with a severe hangover

Ecologist

CLEAN CREEPS   Greenpeace; a.k.a. GREEN CREEPS
ZINC THE MINK   Vandalize a fur coat
SOUP POOP   Waste water
CRAP WITH THE CLAP   Hazardous waste

e.g.—*"We just got this report back from the laboratory. There's a lot of **CRAP WITH THE CLAP** in that **SOUP POOP**."*

DOUBLE DEAL   Recycle
TRASH STASH   Landfill
DROSS SAUCE   Garbage
LUNAR LANDSCAPE   Strip mine
RINSE 'N' VAC   Sewer treatment plant
PINS 'N' NEEDLES   Medical waste
LONG NAP   Extinction
CLUB DRUB   Baby seal hunting

e.g.—*"Those seals are in for a **LONG NAP** if they keep getting **CLUBBED** and **DRUBBED** the way they have been."*

FEED THE WEED   Refuse chemical lawn treatment
SPILL IT 'N' KILL IT   Water and soil pollution
WANTED LIST   Endangered species
MIX 'N' MATCH   Biodiversity
RHESUS PIECES   Experiment using monkeys
RANT & CHANT   Animal rights demonstration
AIR TODAY, GONE TOMORROW (ATGT)   Ozone depletion
BLACK STRAW   Alaskan oil pipeline

e.g.—*"I wouldn't worry about the **BLACK STRAW**; you know what they say: **AIR TODAY, GONE TOMORROW**."*

SHRINKIN 'N' SINKIN   Nuclear meltdown
CLICKING   Radioactive contamination
THINKING IT'S SHRINKING   Brazilian rain forest
WOOD HOODS   Developers
PAVE IT, DON'T SAVE IT   Urban renewal
UNSTUCK THE MUCK   Drain and fill in swamps
STICK DICKS   Loggers
GOOKS WITH HOOKS   Japanese fishermen

e.g.—*"I don't know who's worse, the **STICK DICKS** or the **GOOKS WITH HOOKS**."*

FUDGE   Asbestos insulation material
FOLD   Tear down

e.g.—*"They'll be getting **FUDGE** out of that building for years before they can **FOLD** it."*

BLACK HOLE   Nuclear power plant
NUKE PUKE   Nuclear waste
LEAK   Ozone hole
PERM GERM   Pesticide
BLOODBATH   Red tide
TUNA NO HELPER   Drift net
ELECTRIC POWER SHOWER   Acid rain

BANG 'N' CLANG   Noise pollution
HOT 'N' HEAVY   Greenhouse effect
DEPTH CHARGES   Disposable diapers
TRAP DOOR   Landfill
STOVE   Incinerator

e.g.—*"What happens to the **DEPTH CHARGES** when they close the **TRAP DOOR**? Maybe they'll go back to the **STOVE**."*

FRY 'N' DIE   Global warming
SLOW THE FLOW   Reduce toxic waste
SPILL 'N' KILL   Oil spill
BETTER RED THAN DEAD   Save the Redwood Forest campaign
HITTIN WHILE SITTIN   Violent breakup of a protest demonstration
DECORATE   Vandalize
GRANOLA   Biosphere
BAKE OR BREAK   Biodegradable
GUNS 'N' BOZOS   Heavy metal contaminators
POLLUTER SHOOTER   Violent, radical ecologist

e.g.—*"Those **GUNS 'N' BOZOS** better watch out for the **POLLUTER SHOOTERS**."*

STEAM CREAM   Groundwater contamination
BAGS OF SLAG   Piles of garbage
CLOG OF SMOG   Stationary, heavily polluted air

Fire Fighter

CHOPPER   Ax
HUMP   Pumper
BIG DICK   Ladder truck
PALACE   Firehouse
PULL TOY   Alarm box
PHONY TONY   False alarm
FITs   Felons in training

e.g.—*"Send the **BIG DICK** back to the **PALACE**. It's a **PHONY TONY**. Musta been some **FITs** playing with the **PULL TOY**."*

CHAR THE CAR   Automobile fire
PANTRY PARTY   Kitchen fire
SLIPPERS   Boots
SKULL HULL   Helmet
RUBBER BAND   Fire-retardant coat
MEASLES   Dalmatian dog
SWELTER SHELTER   Tenement building
SHINE LINE   Spotlight
GERONIMO   Fire chief
HOSEHEAD   Fireman
LONG DROP   Hotel fire

e.g.—*"Ask **GERONIMO** how many **HOSEHEADS** he needs at that **LONG DROP**."*

UFO   Undetermined fire origin; a.k.a. UNIDENTIFIED FRIED OBJECT
SHERLOCK   Fire marshal
SHIP CHIP   Boat fire
MICROBE   Rookie fireman
ENVELOPE   Body bag; a.k.a. KNAPSACK

e.g.—*"Have the **MICROBE** bring an **ENVELOPE** to the second-floor porch. We've got a **UFO** up here."*

PLANE FLAME   Airplane crash
PASTA   Foam
ROMAN CANDLE   Explosion
HELL SHELL   Abandoned building
BURN TO EARN   Arson
BLINDERS   Flashing lights
BAD BABY   Siren
SLIDE   Fire escape
CANDLE   Skyscraper
SHOWER   Sprinkler system
TOXIC 'N' CAUSTIC (T 'N' C)   Chemical fire
WRONG GONG   Alarm malfunction

GROW 'N' GLOW   Exposure to hazardous material
PUT IN A SKYLIGHT   Open the roof to vent out toxic fumes

e.g.—*"We got here late because the GONG was WRONG at the CANDLE. Better PUT IN A SKYLIGHT now or they'll be GROWING 'N' GLOWING."*

POOCH POLE   Hydrant
CAN OPENER   Jaws of Life
HIGH 'N' DRY   Insufficient water pressure
SPARK PLUG   Arsonist
EMBER   Person killed in a fire
TYRO PYRO   Child playing with matches
COCONUT GRAVE   Nightclub fire
STOPPED 'N' DROPPED   Patrons overcome at a blocked exit door
SLICK DICK   Nozzle
SCORCHED BY HIS TORCH   Arsonist killed by his own fire

e.g.—*"This guy got SCORCHED BY HIS TORCH. Originally, we thought we had a TYRO PYRO. But SHERLOCK figured out that the EMBER was actually the SPARK PLUG."*

LUNG DUNG   Asbestos insulation material
FRY OR FLY   High-rise fire
SMOKE CHOKE   Killed by fumes
FUME TOMB   Dead by smoke inhalation
BUBBLE TROUBLE   Victim with third-degree burns
PORK STRIPS   Dead burn victims
CRISCO DISCO   Fatal fire in a dance hall
CRISPY CRITTERS   Dead animals

e.g.—*"Lots of CRISPY CRITTERS were left in that CANDLE this morning. How many PORK STRIPS did they find in the CRISCO DISCO last night?"*

Health Club Supervisor

PRESSURE COOKER Steam bath
SUITCASE Gym bag
KEY FEE Membership
SLIM GYM Health spa
TRIM THE LIMBS Lose weight
MICROWAVE Sauna
THONG Female
PRONG Erection

e.g.—*"She's gorgeous. I'd like to put a **PRONG** in that **THONG**."*

SWEATSHOP Fitness center
DREADMILL Treadmill
BROILER Tanning booth
DE SADE Trainer
DEATH MARCH Marathon

e.g.—*"When I leave the **PRESSURE COOKER**, I'll definitely try out that **DREADMILL**."*

GET THAT HOG TO JOG Persuade an obese person to start a running program
JEWEL BOX Athletic supporter
TALKY JOCKEY Attendant
CRANKCASE Bodybuilder
COW CHOW High-carbohydrate diet

e.g.—*"I wonder how much **COW CHOW** that **CRANKCASE** is putting away every day?"*

STEEL MEAL Weight training
TRIPLE PLAY Triathlon
HALF-WIT Biathlete
ERECTION FROM THE REFLECTION Mirror-gazing

e.g.—*"Look at that HALF-WIT in the corner. If he looks at himself any longer, he'll be getting an ERECTION FROM THE REFLECTION."*

TRIP, STUMBLE, & FALL (TS&F)   Exercise
CHEST   Female guest
VEST   Male guest
FRUIT LOOP   Juice bar
LOW BLOW   Minimal impact aerobics
ROWBOAT   Rotary torso machine
SPIKE DYKES   Women's volleyball team

e.g.—*"While we're waiting for that ROWBOAT, let's go watch the SPIKE DYKES."*

STARVE IT OR CARVE IT   Eat less or work out more frequently
HOGS IN TOGS   Fat people in sweatsuits
SPAMDEX   Extra large workout wear

e.g.—*"Those HOGS IN TOGS are really stretching the SPAMDEX. Better get 'em to the DREADMILL."*

DOESN'T LIKE THE BIKE   Client who refuses to work out on the stationary bicycle
CRUNCH COUNTER   Massage table
GHOUL POOL   Whirlpool
PILLAR TO POST   Step aerobics
SLUMPING JACK   Jumping jack
SNAP IT OR FLAP IT   Stretching
BOOGIE BOOTS   Running shoes
FLOGGING TRACK   Jogging track
CRAWL-ATHLETICS   Calisthenics
SORE DICK TRACK   Nordic track
GYM BAG   Dirty, smelly member

e.g.—*"Remind GYM BAG he really needs to get in the PRESSURE COOKER."*

TOWEL BOUNCER   Counter clerk
CRAMP CHAMP   Lap swimmer
SINK   Lap pool

PULLING THE TRAIN   Lifting weights
FREIGHT   Free weights

e.g.—*"Go help the **CRAMP CHAMP** out of the **SINK**. Then see if you can talk him into **PULLING THE TRAIN** today. He can start with the **FREIGHT** first."*

WALK OUT   Workout
HOT TO TROT   Warmed up
WRENCH PRESS   Bench press
BITCH OF A TWITCH   Severe muscle spasm
CRATE SIFTER   Weightlifter
GLUT BUTT   Overweight buttocks
GRIPS ON HIS HIPS   Midriff bulge
CHAINSAW DIET   Plastic surgery

e.g.—*"That **CRATE SIFTER** has got **GRIPS ON HIS HIPS** and a **GLUT BUTT**. He really should get on the **FLOGGING TRACK** right away. About the only thing that's gonna help him is a **CHAINSAW DIET**."*

High School Teacher

SUBTERRANEAN   Slow students; a.k.a. SUB
DROP KICK   Flunk

e.g.—*"I'm gonna have to **DROP KICK** that **SUB**."*

DOPE 'N' GROPE   Prom
FUTURE MORTICIANS OF AMERICA (FMA)   Especially ugly students
DOORSTOP   Janitor
PIPE   Bathroom
ZOO   Pep rally
FRENCHMEN   Freshman students
SOPs   Sophomore students
NITRO   Chem lab
STIR   Detention
MIA   Student on the sick list

COW SWILL   Student council
HAMMERHEADS   Vocational education students
COFFINS   Lockers
ED HEAD   Principal
DYING INSTRUCTOR   Driving instructor
FLOWERPOT   Maintenance person
BARFETERIA   Cafeteria

e.g.—*"The DOORSTOP is looking for a couple of FLOWERPOTS to meet him in the BARFETERIA."*

TATTLER   School newspaper
BEERBOOK   Yearbook
POP 'N' DROP   Drink and drive
FROSTED FLAKE   Cheerleader
SMALL FRY   Juniors
SHRINK THINK   Psychology
CLIT LIT   Feminist literature

e.g.—*"Two SMALL FRY want to transfer from SHRINK THINK to CLIT LIT."*

EAR-BEATERS   Band
ROUNDUP   Student assembly
NERD HERD   Honor society
VAL DICK   Valedictorian; a.k.a. VD
HEADSHOP   Guidance counselor
FERN   Special ed student
ASS PASS   Hall permit
REFUGEE   Transfer student
BUD WEISER   Advisor
BUCKLE ON THE KNUCKLE   Discipline slip

e.g.—*"I've gotta find out why BUD WEISER put the BUCKLE ON Tim's KNUCKLE."*

SCENERY   Seniors
GRAVES   Grades
LIFT-OFF   Graduation
GROANROOM   Homeroom

PAWN Chess club member

e.g.—*"That PAWN wasn't in GROANROOM today."*

GREEK SPEAK Foreign languages
MONGOL HORDE Student body
STAMMER SLAMMER Assembly hall
FARTED Expelled
XEROXING Copying homework
ROCKS IN A BOX Geology
JUMPS 'N' LUMPS Physical education
BRUSHED BACK Suspended
BEANED Received detention
CLASSHOPPER Student who skips classes
DOMEWORK Homework
HOMEWRECK Home economics
STONES Students
NO-NECKS Jocks
BLEACHER CREATURES Hecklers at sporting events

e.g.—*"Did any of the BLEACHER CREATURES get BRUSHED BACK?"*

NO-CLASS ROOM Study hall
DREK TREK Class trip; a.k.a. LIVE DIVE
SOREST Chorus

Hunting Guide

LICENSE TO KILL (LTK) Hunting permit
POCKET CHANGE Small game
RUBBERS Waders
OSWALD High-powered rifle

e.g.—*"You don't need an LTK for POCKET CHANGE. I'm going to get my OSWALD and RUBBERS."*

POP GUN Old hunter
BAG 'N' TAG Kill a game animal

ROUND UP & SHOOT UP (RUSU) Game preserve
SOLD OUT Maximum limit
STAG PARTY Deer hunting
PUMPKIN Orange clothing
BARNS Big game
ANYTHING THAT MOVES (ATM) Open season
MACHINE GUN KELLY Novice hunter

e.g.—*"MACHINE GUN KELLY wants to know if it's ATM yet."*

TONTO Bow-hunter
THUMPER PUMPER Shotgun
BANGER HANGER Gun rack

e.g.—*"Ask TONTO if he left my THUMPER PUMPER on the BANGER HANGER."*

CANNONS IN THE CANYON Shooting blind
QUACKERS Ducks
GUN BUN Holster
INTENT ON THE SCENT Tracking
BRANDO Elephant gun
ELVIS Hound dog

e.g.—*"Before ELVIS gets INTENT ON THE SCENT, I've gotta get my BRANDO outta the GUN BUN."*

RUGS Animal pelts
HUNS WITH GUNS Hunting party
HOUND 'N' IMPOUND Wildlife management
COYOTE COP Game warden
HACKSAW Taxidermist
FIT 'N' SIT Stuff and mount a dead animal
FOX IN THE BOX Spring trap
STEAL THE VEAL Poach
SNATCH 'N' DISPATCH Trap and kill small animals
WELCOME MAT No-trespassing sign
OPEN FOR BUSINESS Dress out a dead animal
BULLWINKLE Moose
SLICE IT 'N' ICE IT Skin and freeze an animal

RUNNY BUNNY   Eviscerated rabbit

e.g.—*"Whaddaya gonna do with that RUNNY BUNNY? SLICE IT 'N' ICE IT?"*

BULLET BAIT   Nonhunters in the woods
LEAD IN THE HEAD   Accidentally shot; a.k.a. CRACK IN THE BACK, HIT
   IN THE TIT

e.g.—*"BULLET BAIT better get out of here before he gets some LEAD IN THE HEAD."*

ROUND IN THE HOUND   Accidental shooting of a domestic animal
WAIT AT THE GATE   Set out a lure
SIT STILL 'N' KILL   Ambush prey that's been driven toward the hunter
PUT A HOLE IN THE MOLE   Varmint shooting
FARMER   Landowner
WRAP THE SCRAPS   Dispose of the carcass
BAMBI BURGER   Venison

e.g.—*"I think we've got enough BAMBI BURGERS now. Let's WRAP THE SCRAPS. Maybe the FARMER will let us PUT SOME HOLES IN HIS MOLES on the way out."*

PERISCOPE   Telescopic sight
QADDAFI   Duck decoy
BOYZ IN THE WOODS   Hunters
BUSTED COMPASS   Guide
BOUGHT IT 'N' SHOT IT   Buy and shoot previously captured game animal
NEXT COUNTY   Shoot from a long distance
SHOT IN BED   Shot at point-blank range
BLOTTO OTTO   Drunken hunter

e.g.—*"He wasn't in the NEXT COUNTY when he put a ROUND IN THE HOUND. Even a BLOTTO OTTO wouldn't have SHOT HIM IN BED."*

Mortician

ROAD KILL   Any client killed in a highway accident; a.k.a. FLAP JACK, TORSO EXPANSION, FRISBEE, PAVEMENT PRINCESS (female), HIGHWAY MARKER (male)

PIZZA   Victim smashed beyond recognition in a motor vehicle collision or a suicide from a tall building; a.k.a. STRAWBERRY SUNDAE, GOOEY LOUIE, or STICKEY NICKY (male); GAMY AMY or LEAPIN LENA (female)

e.g.—*"Maloney is definitely gonna be a closed casket job. He PIZZAED from the top of the Commerce Bank Building late last night."*

SHAKER   Clients who suffer involuntary postmortem muscle spasm; a.k.a. JACK IN THE BOX, NOMAD; CHUCK BERRY or JAMES BROWN (African-American)

POTATO CHIP (PC) WHACKER   Bulimic client who, during the act of purging, chokes on the vomit and expires

e.g.—*"I had to go collect a young college girl who had scarfed down three sixteen-ounce PC bags before WHACKING herself out in the upstairs bathroom."*

SWISS CHEESED   Shot at close range by someone using a powerful automatic weapon

SUNUNUED   To be killed in a clumsy, heavy-handed, vengeful way; a.k.a. NIXONED

e.g.—*"When her husband caught her in bed with the Democratic gubernatorial candidate, they both got SUNUNUED with a baseball bat."*

BOXCAR   Hearse; a.k.a. ROACH COACH, DEPART CART, SLAB CAB

MARLA MAPLES   Well-endowed female corpse; earlier known as MARILYN MONROE or RAQUEL WELCH

MARIE ANTOINETTE   Headless corpse; a.k.a. JAYNE MANSFIELD

ANKLE BRACELETS   Short leg-irons applied to especially attractive corpses so as to prevent sexual activity

FLATLINE JUMPER   Necrophiliac

47

FLATLINE QUICKIE   Necrophilia; a.k.a. DEAD HEAD

e.g.—*"Better put the **ANKLE BRACELETS** on that **MARLA MAPLES**. Chet's parking the **BOXCAR** and he's probably looking for a little **FLATLINE QUICKIE**."*

CHANGE PURSE   Body bag; a.k.a. ZIPLOC, SLOUCH POUCH, FACE CASE
DOGGIE BAG   Deceased found in several places
HALF 'N' HALF   Victim that's been bisected, usually at a construction site, railroad crossing, or intersection collision

e.g.—*"Gimme a hand and we'll haul this **PIZZA** outta the **CHANGE PURSE**. Then I've gotta grab a **HALF 'N' HALF** near the Amtrak station."*

PRUNE   Severely dehydrated corpse
NEUTRON BOMB   AIDS victim

e.g.—*"I'd rather retrieve a pair of week-old rooming house **PRUNES** than a **NEUTRON BOMB** any day."*

EXXON VALDEZ   Badly leaking client; a.k.a. PUDDLE, BAD ALIBI
MONA LISA   Severely disfigured victim who requires an extraordinary amount of care and attention
MORGUE JOCKEY   Apprentice mortician; a.k.a. GHOUL

e.g.—*"That **MONA LISA**'s puddling all over the casket liner again. Tell that **MORGUE JOCKEY** to bring the quick plug and a trowel!"*

ZEPPELIN   Fat client; a.k.a. ORSON WELLES, ORSON, DELTA BURKE, BEACH BALL
HINDENBURG   Fat victim killed in a gas explosion
CHARCOAL   Burn victim; a.k.a. CINDER, SMOKER, ZIPPO
BYE-BYE BASKET   Casket
ROLLS-ROYCE   Expensive mahogany casket
PINTO   Cheap, cloth-covered pine box
SUNNY-SIDE UP   Open-casket wake
SLAMMED THE DOOR   Closed-coffin service
NAPALM   Cremation
ASHTRAY   Cremation urn
BEAUTY PARLOR   Preparation room for embalming

e.g.—*"While you're moving that ZEPPELIN into the BEAUTY PARLOR, I'll drop the SMOKER in the BYE-BYE BASKET. What a waste. The family should just NAPALM the rest of him and flick him into an ASHTRAY!"*

BULL'S-EYE   Mob informant killed in the Federal Witness Protection Program

e.g.—*"Grab a couple of ZIPLOCS, because that call was from the FBI. They just found two BULL'S-EYES in the trunk of a rented car out at the airport."*

WOODPECKER   Inept embalmer; a.k.a. DRIBBLER
SINKER   Drowning victim
TITANIC   Fat drowning victim
WORM WORLD   Cemetery or mausoleum; a.k.a. DUSTBIN
MEAT MARKET   Morgue
SLICE 'N' DICE   Autopsy; a.k.a. CHOP 'N' LOP, STAB 'N' SLAB, HACK 'N' STACK, CUT 'N' GUT, REND 'N' SEND, AMPUTATE 'N' EXCAVATE
SWINGER   Hanging victim; a.k.a. ROPE DOPE

e.g.—*"After I unload this TITANIC at WORM WORLD, we can snatch the SWINGER at the MEAT MARKET."*

GREEN CHEESE   Badly decomposed body
BISCUIT   Gravestone
HOLE IN ONE   Suicide by shooting; a.k.a. BRAIN DRAIN
LAST SUPPER   Poisoning victim
SHOULDER BAIT   Grief counseling

e.g.—*"Bring Mrs. Smith in the office for some SHOULDER BAIT. Then she can pick out a BISCUIT for the LAST SUPPER."*

PILL KILL   Fatal drug overdose
POP FLY   Victim, high on drugs, took a fatal plunge out of a window or off a roof
SCORECARD   Obituary notice
GRAND SLAM   An entire family dies in a common disaster such as a plane crash or train wreck; a.k.a. LOTTO TICKET

e.g.—*"This place was a real zoo last night. First we had a POP FLY from the thirtieth floor of the Chrysler Building. Two hours later we lucked out* with a **GRAND SLAM** *from that jumbo jet crash at JFK. Go ahead and call the newspaper and give 'em the* **SCORECARD.**"

SLAB GAB   Eulogy
GO SHOW   Funeral
WAKE HIM UP   Exhume the body
TABLECLOTH   Shroud
GRUESOME TWOSOME   Murder and suicide
WHO OWNS THE BONES   Dispute over possession of the corpse
GRUESOME TOOTHSOME   Suicide by shooting in the mouth
CARCASS FROM CARACAS   Funeral arrangements for an overseas victim
SOREHEAD   Crushed victim
PARADE   Funeral cortege or procession
ENTERTAIN THE REMAINS   Prepare the body for viewing
DEAD BED   Grave site
CHAR BAR   Crematory

e.g.—*"Time to get that* **CARCASS FROM CARACAS.** *No need to* **ENTERTAIN THE REMAINS.** *She's going to the* **CHAR BAR.**"

SWEETBREAD   Viscera
HOME ALONE   No bodies in the funeral home
KEVORKIAN   Public relations firm specializing in funeral homes

e.g.—*"Things are really slow around here. I've been* **HOME ALONE** *for the past week. Maybe I'll hire* **KEVORKIAN.**"

SHOW TIME   Visiting hours
MACKEREL   Victim who froze to death
BOAT FLOAT   Burial at sea; a.k.a. SHIP DRIP
QUICK KICK   Died suddenly
SPADE BRIGADE   Gravediggers

Nuclear Power Plant Operator

MISSING LINKS   Nuclear Regulatory Commission
TIME BOMB   Nuclear power plant
LEFTOVERS   Spent nuclear fuel
SKILLET   Storage
SCAN THE CAN   Inspect

e.g.—*"Put the LEFTOVERS in the SKILLET for now. The MISSING LINKS are coming over to SCAN THE CAN."*

COOK THE BROOK   Discharge radioactive water
LEAD HEAD   Plant operator

e.g.—*"That LEAD HEAD is in big trouble. He just COOKED THE BROOK."*

SCREAM GENERATOR   Steam generator
ALARM CLOCK   Radiation monitor
QUACK SHACK   Security office
LICENSE TO DIE (LTD)   Full power permit
CRYPT   Nuclear reactor
FELT HIS BELT MELT   Aware of a runaway reaction
VAPORIZE THOSE GUYS   Core meltdown
BEIJING SURPRISE   China syndrome
RABBIT   Breeder reactor
BIG BLOW   Megawatt
THREE MILES HIGH   Three Mile Island power plant
AMMO   Fuel rods
TANNING BOOTH   Reactor vessel
SELF-DESTRUCT   Chain reaction

e.g.—*"Better get more AMMO over to the TANNING BOOTH. They're ready to SELF-DESTRUCT again."*

NO CRANIUM   Uranium
SPLIT THE SHIT   Nuclear fusion

RUSSIAN ROULETTE   Chernobyl meltdown
FIREFLY   Radiation victim
PUCE JUICE   Nuclear-generated electricity
BOOMER TUMORS   Cancer
THREE-HEADED COWS   Birth defects
STEAM BATH   Radiation leak
FRIGHT SWITCH   Automatic shutdown

e.g.—*"Ever since last month's STEAM BATH, the MISSING LINKS have been out looking for THREE-HEADED COWS. There would be a lot more BOOMER TUMORS if the FRIGHT SWITCH didn't work."*

KILLER WADS   Kilowatts
OVERKILL   Excess capacity
PLUGGED IN   On-line

e.g.—*"That RABBIT is gonna produce mucho KILLER WADS when it gets PLUGGED IN."*

SHIT HIT   Contaminated
SHIT CLICKER   Geiger counter
SAP   Subatomic particles
OOZIN 'N' LOSIN   Pipe cracking
BAGGIES   Waste containers
KRYPTONITE   Lead clothing
BURN IT PERMIT   Temporary license
SHOOT 'N' BOOT   Decommission expense
BLOWING 'N' GLOWING   Radioactive
NERVOUS TILL IT'S OUT OF SERVICE   Satisfied when decommissioned
LEAD SHED   Containment building
EMPTY GUN   Spent fuel
BLOWOUT   Fusion
COOK   Reprocessed fuel
REQUIEM MASS   Critical mass; a.k.a. CRITICAL LIST
VICTIMS   Visitors

e.g.—*"The VICTIMS want to know what time REQUIEM MASS starts."*

TUCK IT 'N' TRUCK IT   Transport nuclear waste
TOP GLOP   High-level waste
LOOK 'N' COOK   Guided tour
LABEL ON THE TABLE   Visitor's pass

Nurse

ROADBLOCK   Constipated patient
POPPER   Enema; a.k.a. RIPCORD
SCOREBOARD   Chart

e.g.—*"Look at that **ROADBLOCK**'s **SCOREBOARD**. It's time for a **POPPER**."*

FRIDGE   Dead on arrival (DOA)
COLLAR   Chaplain
NUTHOUSE   Emergency room (ER)
TOMAHAWK   Neurosurgeon
DOME COMB   Brain scan
GAMMA JAMMA   X-rays
3MI (THREE MILE ISLAND)   Radiology
VAMPIRE   Patient with AIDS
BRAIN PAIN   Headache
ZOMBIE   Orderly

e.g.—*"The **VAMPIRE**'s got a **BRAIN PAIN**. **TOMAHAWK** wants a **ZOMBIE** to take him to **3MI** for **GAMMA JAMMA** and a **DOME COMB**."*

CHOP SHOP   Operating room; a.k.a. DOWNTOWN
SWINE LINE   Menu; a.k.a. LAST RITES
MORGUE   Cafeteria
RATCHED   Head nurse; a.k.a. WRETCHED
PAPER TRAIL   Records
CASH 'N' CARRY   Billing office
HOLDUP   Operation
GRAB   Admit
BLACK TONGUE   Very sick patient

*e.g.—"RATCHED says we should check the **PAPER TRAIL** at **CASH 'N'
CARRY** before we **GRAB** that **BLACK TONGUE**."*

COUGH DROP   Ear, nose, and throat specialist
SNEEZY   Allergist
DEEP SIX   Patient with severe breathing problems
MINER   Emphysema patient
FIVE ALARM   Fever
HOP 'N' POP   Suffer a stroke
CHECK THE OIL   Take temperature and vital signs

*e.g.—"I'll **CHECK THE MINER'S OIL**. I think he's got a **FIVE ALARM**."*

DOORBELL   Patient who frequently rings the buzzer
PRICK STICK   Needle
BRAIN DRAIN   Lobotomy

*e.g.—"If that **DOORBELL** keeps it up, I'm going to give him a **PRICK
STICK** and send him **DOWNTOWN** for a **BRAIN DRAIN**."*

HUMPTY DUMPTY   Trauma victim
BONEHEAD   Orthopedist
RACK   Traction
LOG   Cast
GOLD MINE   Patient with a lot of problems
CAVEMAN   Obstetrician-gynecologist
BABY DROPPER   Maternity patient
WOMB BROOM   Hysterectomy
DREAM TEAM   Anesthesiologists

*e.g.—"**CAVEMAN** wants to schedule a **WOMB BROOM** on the **BABY
DROPPER**. You call the **DREAM TEAM**."*

MITT   Bedpan
LUMPY   Patient with hemorrhoids
CRUST   Bedsore
JAM   Ointment

*e.g.—"**LUMPY** wants some **JAM** for his **CRUST** and a new **MITT**."*

RHUMBA   Experience cardiac arrest

HOP 'N' FLOP   Treadmill test
BLOOD FLOOD   Hemorrhage
GRAVE ROB   Resuscitate; a.k.a. WIND THE CLOCK
TWIST 'N' SHOUT   Convulse; a.k.a. POP THE CLUTCH
CLOSE TO DEAD (CTD)   Intensive care unit
BLACK TUESDAY   Die

e.g.—*"Fenwick began to RHUMBA on the HOP 'N' FLOP at the same time Mrs. Smith POPPED HER CLUTCH and started a BLOOD FLOOD. We had to WIND Fenwick's CLOCK just to get him into CTD. I hope he doesn't BLACK TUESDAY on us."*

HEAD SHOP   Psychiatric wing
JUNKYARD   Pharmacy
REAGANITIS   Alzheimer's disease
CATNAP   Cataleptic patient
MONEY BUNNY   Doctor
STAT   Demanding, complaining patient
DRIP   Intravenous tube
SHAKE 'N' BAKE   Radiation treatment
PORK CHOP   Vasectomy
DICK DOC   Urologist
CORN CUTTER   Podiatrist

e.g.—*"Nancy's new up here. Introduce her to the CORN CUTTER while I set up a PORK CHOP for the DICK DOC."*

NO TAN   Anemic patient
BUG DRUG   Antibiotics
COCK POX   Venereal disease
KILLED IN ACTION (KIA)   Medical malpractice suit
HOOKED IT   Made the wrong diagnosis; a.k.a. SLICED IT
SNAP, CRACKLE, & POP   Osteoporosis patient
MANUAL LABOR   Physical therapy
POTTY JOCKEY   Patient with diarrhea
ZIPPER   Sutures
JUMP START   CPR
HANDOUT   Welfare patient
FAKER   Hypochondriac

PUS BUS   Ambulance
FOOTBALL HIM TO A TIN CUP   Dump a patient in a charity hospital

e.g.—*"I still think that HANDOUT's a FAKER. Call the PUS BUS and we'll FOOTBALL HIM TO A TIN CUP."*

DIRECT TRAFFIC   Assign patients
IGOR   Intern
LAVA LAMP   Leper
NORIEGA   Dermatologist
LIGHT ZORRO   Laser surgeon
GORBACHEV   Port wine stain

e.g.—*"That IGOR certainly doesn't know how to DIRECT TRAFFIC. Send the LAVA LAMP to NORIEGA. Then have a ZOMBIE take GORBACHEV to the LIGHT ZORRO."*

SLEEPER   Coma victim
BLOOD BUCKET   Hemophiliac
QUAYLE THE RECIPE   Misread the chart
GERALDO   Cause brain damage

e.g.—*"Make sure the TOMAHAWK doesn't QUAYLE THE BLOOD BUCKET'S RECIPE and GERALDO her."*

BROKEN EGGSHELL   Fractured skull
SHARP CURVE   Scoliosis patient
CHAINSAW   Orthopedic surgeon

e.g.—*"Tell CHAINSAW he has a SHARP CURVE in the CHOP SHOP."*

PINHEAD   Acupuncturist
CHIROQUACKTOR   Chiropractor
SPINE OUTTA LINE   Degenerative disc disease

e.g.—*"Although his SPINE'S OUTTA LINE, he'd be better off going to a PINHEAD than a CHIROQUACKTOR."*

FULL MOON   Crowded emergency room
BOFFO CASH REGISTER   Busy billing department
LEMON   Jaundice
DRIBBLER   Neurologically impaired patient

RIDE INSIDE   Visit to the internist

e.g.—*"I definitely think the **LEMON DRIBBLER** ought to go for a **RIDE INSIDE**."*

HERB   Naturopathic doctor
CURB   Suspend the hospital privileges
ROOTS   Herbal medicine
PUTTER   Club foot
SPIDERMEN   Siamese twins
RUTHLESS 'N' TOOTHLESS   Irritable older patient
PILLOW PUSHER   Euthanasia advocate

e.g.—*"If **RUTHLESS 'N' TOOTHLESS** keeps aggravating me, I'm gonna send a **PILLOW PUSHER** to her room."*

MESS ON THE STRESS   Poor performance on the stress test; a.k.a. TEST
   WAS A MESS
ROCK IN HIS CLOCK   Heart blockage
DETOUR   Heart bypass operation
SLIDE OUTSIDE   C-section
INTERIOR DECORATING   D&C
DRAINPIPE   Colostomy bag

Nursing Home Operator

GRAVY TRAIN   Medical and health insurance
GOLD TOOTH   Medicare benefits
FOOD STAMP   Public assistance patient
SANTA   Welfare department

e.g.—*"Tell **SANTA** we're not interested in that **FOOD STAMP**."*

TELLER   Accounting department
BANK   Nursing home
ATM   Bed
FISHHEADS   Special diet
25-WATTER   Nurse's aid

ROT POT   Dining room
PEANUT BRITTLE   Bedsore
WORST   Nurse
EINSTEIN   Doctor

e.g.—*"EINSTEIN was here a minute ago. He wants a WORST to go check out that PEANUT BRITTLE on Mr. Henderson."*

SPIDER   Walker
BAT   Cane
GO-CART   Wheelchair
GOING AWAY PARTY (GAP)   Last rites
SPRINTER   Stroke victim
SIT 'N' SHIT   Bedpan
WOOFER   Hearing aid
LOOSE JUICE   Laxative
SLINKY   Patient with Alzheimer's disease
ATTIC   Sheltered care

e.g.—*"That SLINKY doesn't need a BANK. He needs an ATTIC."*

BLUE 'DO   Beauty salon
BOUNCER   Orderly
FIRST GRADE   Speech therapy
GESTAPO   Physical therapy assistants
STRETCH & SCREAM   Physical therapy
BUBBLER   Whirlpool
NUMBER PUMPERS   Clerks in the accounting department
BEDSORES   Consumer watchdog organization
TAB   Monthly statement

e.g.—*"Tell the NUMBER PUMPERS to watch out. A BEDSORE is gonna come over next week to check out the TABS."*

PULP 'N' GULP   Medication time
SIT 'N' KNIT   Arts and crafts
CATTLE CAR   Elevator
PILL BILLS   Fees
CRAM 'N' JAM   Adding additional capacity
DRAPE   Housecoat

SKATES   Slippers
GYP JOINT   Gift shop
CRAWL & FALL   Fire drill

e.g.—*"If there's a CRAWL & FALL, make sure the GO-CARTS are kept out of the CATTLE CAR."*

STIR   Total patient population
JOKE BOOK   State nursing home regulations
MIRANDA WARNINGS   Nursing home patients' bill of rights
FANG GANG   Dentures
BRAN PLAN   Special diet
PRISONER   Resident
DEAF REFS   Complaint board
HAG WITH DRAG   Administrator

e.g.—*"The HAG WITH DRAG told the PRISONER if she doesn't like it, she can go see the DEAF REFS."*

ROAST HOST   Social director
HENHOUSE   Recreation room
SNUFF   Discharge
LATERAL   Transfer

e.g.—*"The TELLER said we should either SNUFF the PRISONER or LATERAL her to another BANK."*

BARE CARE   Personal needs

Pharmacist

TABLE LEAPER   Customer looking for over-the-counter medication
BEANBAG   Truss
JOY JUICE   Cough syrup

e.g.—*"Sam, go help that TABLE LEAPER over in aisle three. He's looking for a BEANBAG and some JOY JUICE."*

POP THE CORK   Fill the prescription

TRIPPED ON SCRIPT   Fooled by a bogus prescription
BRAKE   Tranquilizer
STUTTER   Nervous customer
NAPE DRAPE   Neck brace
SCAFFOLD   Splint
BABY BLEACH   Contraceptive foam
JAM DAM   Spermicidal jelly
ROADBLOCK   Diaphragm; a.k.a. CUM DRUM
COAT   Condom
SPERM SPOUT   IUD
BRONCO BREATH   Halitosis

e.g.—*"Talk to Mrs. Smith. Explain the advantages and disadvantages of a* **COAT, ROADBLOCK, BABY BLEACH,** *and* **JAM DAM.** *Watch out for her, though, she's got* **BRONCO BREATH.**"

ABCs   Vitamins
BABY BUSTER   Birth control pills
DRANO   Laxative
DREAMIN OF SEMEN   Fear of pregnancy
CANDY   Insulin
SICK STICK   Hypodermic needle
SHOCK TROOPER   Diabetic patient
HULK   Steroid user; a.k.a. ARNOLD
CLAWS IN GAUZE   Hand bandage
DRINK 'N' DIE (DND)   Rubbing alcohol
WAKE-UP CALL   Ammonia
POKE STICK   Pair of crutches
HAND BAND   Sling
BLANKET   Sanitary napkin
STOPPER   Tampon
EAR STEER   Cotton swab
JUICE SLUICE   Decongestant
SLIP 'N' SLIDE   Petroleum jelly
BARBIE   Barbiturate
DOZE   Sedative
PILLOWS   Sleeping pills
CLIPPED THE SCRIPT   Stole a prescription

PILL FILL   Legitimate prescription

e.g.—*"Uh-oh, here comes Mrs. Byron. You're probably going to have to POP THE CORK for a BARBIE. Make sure she hasn't CLIPPED THE SCRIPT for some PILLOWS. I don't think she's got a PILL FILL."*

LOG LEG   Prosthesis
RED TAG   Iodine
HOPALONG   Leg amputee
CHINK DRINK   Opiate
FLOPSTER   Narcoleptic
SCUBA DIVER   Bottled-oxygen customer
HACK ATTACK   Coughing fit
CHEW SPEW   Expectorant
PROSTATE WAND   Rubber glove
BUTTONS   Drugs
HOLLOW POINT   Placebo
NAP   Narcotic drug
CLINTON   Inhalant
BALLOON BRAIN   Stuffed-up customer

e.g.—*"Get a CLINTON for the BALLOON BRAIN."*

BRIDGE BOLTER   Depressant
SICK QUICK   Adverse reaction

e.g.—*"Mrs. Smith's gonna get SICK QUICK if she takes the BRIDGE BOLTER and the CHINK DRINK at the same time."*

THROAT COAT   Cough drop
POX IN THE BOX   Yeast infection; a.k.a. FOX WITH THE POX
CAVE WAVE   Douche
SNORT CATCHER   Infant's nasal syringe

Plastic Surgeon

SCRATCH   Perform simple surgery
HATCHET   Surgical tools
FIX AL CAPONE   Revise a scar
CLOSE THE NOSE   Rhinoplasty
HOOK 'N' PULL   Tissue expander
CHOPSTICK   Scalpel

e.g.—*"It's time to **CLOSE THE NOSE**. Get me my **CHOPSTICK** and the **HOOK 'N' PULL**."*

POUCH SLOUCH   Bags under the eyes
TREASURE CHEST   Pectoral implant
MICHAEL JACKSON   Patient who repeatedly seeks plastic surgery
SLICE 'N' SPLICE   Face-lift; a.k.a. RIP 'N' STRIP
CUT 'N' PASTE   Body sculpting
COCK SWAP   Penile implant
NAUGAHYDE   Repeated but unsuccessful surgical tucks

e.g.—*"I had a **MICHAEL JACKSON** in here last week who wanted a **CUT 'N' PASTE**, **SLICE 'N' SPLICE**, and a **COCK SWAP**. He looked like a **NAUGAHYDE** sofa."*

PACK THE CRACK   Collagen injection
DEAD WHALE   Morbidly obese patient
LET SOME AIR OUT   Perform a breast reduction

e.g.—*"It's gonna take a while to **PACK THE CRACK** and **LET SOME AIR OUT** of that **DEAD WHALE**."*

PENGUIN   Patient with webbed feet or toes
DENT IN HIS TENT   Pronounced skull depression
MOUTH IS GOING SOUTH   Obvious harelip

e.g.—*"The **PENGUIN**'s got a **DENT IN HIS TENT** and part of his **MOUTH IS GOING SOUTH**."*

SUB ON THE STUB   Prosthesis
FLAT TIRE   Badly done breast reduction
CLEAVELAND   Clinic
CLIP HER LIP   Repair a cleft lip
SUCK THE MUCK   Liposuction
BURY THE HATCHET   Do extensive, multiple procedures
STAB THE FLAB   Tummy tuck
DRAG THE NET   Stretch and suture wrinkled tissue
REPLACE THE FACE   Chemical peel

e.g.—*"I don't know if we can just REPLACE THE FACE. Maybe we'll have to DRAG THE NET."*

SWELLIN MELON   Breast implant
PLASTER   Silicone
RAG   Dressing
HARVEST SOME CHEST   Remove salvageable skin from a cadaver
STAMP   Skin graft

e.g.—*"Call the lab and tell them we'll have to HARVEST SOME CHEST for that STAMP."*

PUSS 'N' BOOBS   A patient interested in both facial surgery and breast augmentation
BONKERS FOR HONKERS   Approved for breast implant
PUT ON A NEW ROOF   Surgically repair a cleft palate
DISHWASHER   Sterilization machine
SUMP PUMP   Draining wound
BELT SANDER   Dermabrasion tool
FEMUR FROM A LEMUR   Bone graft from an animal
BENT   Severe bone deformity
HAMMER   Local anesthetic
SEW A NEW ROW   Attach a skin flap
BITCH TO STITCH   Hard to suture

e.g.—*"This guy's leg was BENT so bad, we had to get a FEMUR FROM A LEMUR. Get me a HAMMER so I can SEW A NEW ROW. This is going to be a BITCH TO STITCH."*

GOBBLE   Turkey neck

BAGS OF SAGS   Stretch marks

FLYING CARPET   Hair transplant

AX   Surgeon

SHAKE IT 'N' STAKE IT   Ear reattachment

DOUGHNUT BUTT   Big buttocks

TWO BAGGER   Double chin

BLUBBER BANK   Fat deposit

e.g.—*"This guy's a major **BLUBBER BANK**. For starters, he's got a **TWO BAGGER** and a **DOUGHNUT BUTT**. We'll be **CUTTING 'N' PASTING** all afternoon."*

JIGSAW   Difficult reconstructive surgery

OOZE ON A CRUISE   Spreading infection

FAT VAT   Cellulite

VACUUM   Suction

HOG LOGS   Heavy thighs

EYES REVISE   Eyelid tuck

PUB TUB   Beer belly

FRANKENSTEIN   Patient with many facial sutures

WELD   Staple

SUE CREW   Malpractice attorneys

FLOG TAGS   Board certification

e.g.—*"He did a lousy job of **WELDING** that guy's wrist. No wonder the **SUE CREW** is all over him. Wait until they find out he doesn't even have his **FLOG TAGS**."*

Police Supervisor

CRASH 'N' CARRY   Break, enter, and burglarize

BIG TIME CRIME (BTC)   Felony

TREAT LIKE A KING   Beat suspect(s) during an arrest

SHOWED 'EM THE MENU   Read Miranda warning

e.g.—*"We **SHOWED 'EM THE MENU** after **TREATING HIM LIKE A KING**."*

GROIN SOCCER   Physical abuse during interrogation
DOG DIDDLERS   Defense lawyers

e.g.—*"Those **DOG DIDDLERS** want the case dismissed because we played a little **GROIN SOCCER** with that guy."*

FLASH THE CASH   Make bail
SPRAY 'N' PLAY   Mace
SPARKY   Arsonist
POP THE TOP   Bank robbery
KIDDIE KOPS   Juvenile officers
CRACK SNACK   Drug buy
DROP A COP   Assault and battery on a policeman
KICK IN THE DICK   Subdue a suspect

e.g.—*"When you **DROP A COP**, you have to expect a **KICK IN THE DICK**."*

DUCK   Squad car
RACE 'N' MACE   High-speed pursuit
ANKLE JERK   Foot patrolman; a.k.a. HEEL
SWERVIN MERVIN   Drunk driver

e.g.—*"Some **ANKLE JERK** lost a **SWERVIN MERVIN** until we **RACED 'N' MACED** him."*

PISS 'N' MOANER   Misdemeanor
REVEAL THE EEL   Expose oneself; a.k.a. GRAND OPENING
KLEENEX   Vagrant

e.g.—*"Has that **KLEENEX** got a **DOG DIDDLER** yet?"*

MASTER BLASTER   Mob hit man
LOCKSMITH   Bondsman
GRAB 'N' GROPE   Sexual battery
DUMB ASS   Prosecutor
GRUDGE   Judge
FOLLOWING TOO CLOSE   Indecent exposure
NAP 'N' TRAP   Stakeout
MAUSER IN HIS TROUSER   Concealed weapon; a.k.a. ROCKET IN HIS
    POCKET

AIDS BOTTLE   Prostitute

DOFF 'N' COUGH   Strip search; a.k.a. COPE THE DOPE

PROCTO COP   Internal affairs investigator

BARE-ASSED   Off-duty

DEB BALL   Roll call

LOOK 'N' BOOK   Search and seizure

BAD HAT   Pimp

QUARTER HORSE   Meter maid

DEAD DOC   Coroner

HUNK IN THE TRUNK   Shooting victim concealed in a car truck

e.g.—*"DEAD DOC says the HUNK IN THE TRUNK's been dead for three days."*

HIDE 'N' SLIDE   Shoplift

BUDGE THE JUDGE   Obtain a warrant

DEADBEAT   Homicide division

STICK UP THE PICKUP   Auto theft; a.k.a. DISLODGE THE DODGE

BASH 'N' TRASH   Vandalize

ASSAULT THE VAULT   Crack a safe

HIT LIST   Witness

COAST 'N' TOAST   Drive-by shooting

e.g.—*"Have they got a HIT LIST on that COAST 'N' TOAST?"*

MAMAS 'N' PAPAS   Crime family

LEAD SINGER   Gang leader

KNIFE IN THE WIFE   Domestic disturbance; a.k.a. GROOM IN THE TOMB

SCURVY   Jury

BUSHWACKER   Date rape

CARESS   Arrest

DEFECTIVE   Detective

WALL-HOPPER   Fugitive

MOUNTAINMEN   State police

e.g.—*"Those MOUNTAINMEN sent over the DEFECTIVE to CARESS that WALL-HOPPER."*

WIMPS 'N' PIMPS   Civilian review board

LOW-PRICE CLODS   Vice squad

PUT A GUN ON THE NUN   False arrest; a.k.a. PUT A ROPE ON THE POPE

e.g.—*"Who **PUT A GUN ON THE NUN**? Was it those **LOW-PRICE CLODS**?"*

SIT 'N' LIE   Testify
IMPOSSIBLE LAWS   Probable cause
BLACK 'N' BLUE   Minority officer
PRIME CRIME   Peak time for criminal activity

e.g.—*"Besides the **BLACK 'N' BLUE**, who's working **PRIME CRIME** tonight?"*

TRANSVESTITE   Undercover cop
POKE THE COKE   Drug bust
GRIEF   Police chief; a.k.a. MIS-CHIEF
BIKE DYKE   Female motorcycle cop
CHOPPER COPPER   Male motorcycle cop
WINDOW WARMER   Voyeur
MAID IN THE SHADE   Exhibitionist

e.g.—*"The **CHOPPER COPPER** didn't know who to arrest, the **MAID IN THE SHADE** or the **WINDOW WARMER**."*

Postal Worker

BLOW SHEET   Franked mail
LANDFILL   Circulars
HERNIA TIME   Publisher's Clearing House delivery
FARGO CARGO   Holding area for nonessential mail

e.g.—*"Uh-oh, I see it's **HERNIA TIME** again. Get that **LANDFILL** outta the bus and put the **BLOW SHEETS** into the **FARGO CARGO**."*

PETER PRINCIPLE   Seniority
SHOTGUNNED   Transferred
PAN 'N' SCAN   Mail sorter machine
WRAP   Hold order

TRUNDLE THE BUNDLE   To forward mail

STOLE HOLE   Post office box

ALCATRAZ   Post office

OBIT PIT   Dead-letter area

PIANO   Large package

HARD TIME   Customer window service; a.k.a. IN THE HOLE

SLACK STACK   Badly wrapped packages

FURNACE FUEL   Letters to Santa Claus

PUT TO SLEEP   Destroy unaddressed or lost mail

e.g.—*"Here, put this **SLACK STACK** in the **OBIT PIT** for now. I'll **WRAP** this **FURNACE FUEL** until we **PUT IT TO SLEEP**."*

CRACK   Mail slot

ROOFED IT   Left the package on someone's roof

ROPE A DOPE   Mail scams

DATE BAIT   Introduction service scam

BEG BAG   Religious requests for money; a.k.a. CURE LURE

KGB   Postal inspectors

HAIR CURLERS   Complaints

GIN BIN   Collection box

HEARSE   Delivery truck

LEPERS   Nonunion help

BLIND LEPERS   Nonunion temporary help

e.g.—*"Get those **LEPERS** to clean out the **HEARSE**. I've got three more **GIN BINS** to empty this morning."*

MAIL-IT MANIA   Christmas rush

SEWER SERVICE   Getting rid of second- and third-class mail

LICKER   Stamp collector

CHARGE CARD   Postage meter

COUNTER MOUNTER   Customer

PROMOTED   Fired

NOISE BOX   Barking dog

HERMIT   Pen pal

COAL MINE   Delivery route

DRAFT NOTICE   Registered mail

RELIC   Customer who takes a long time at the window

ONE-ARMED BANDIT   Stamp machine
GRILL   Weighing scale
TAMPER   Overcharge a customer

e.g.—*"We need some help out here. You go take the* **RELIC** *with the* **DRAFT NOTICE** *while I fix this* **ONE-ARMED BANDIT**. *Put it on the* **GRILL** *before you* **TAMPER** *with it."*

IQ   Zip code
LOW IQ   Incorrect zip code
ORPHAN   Piece of lost mail
GOOD BOOK   Zip code directory
CHINESE WATER TORTURE (CWT)   Grievance procedure
REAMSTERS   Postal workers' union; a.k.a. DREAMSTERS
DR. WU   Administrative law judge at a grievance hearing

e.g.—*"There's a* **CWT** *tonight for Watson. The* **KGB** *wants* **DR. WU** *to* **PROMOTE** *him."*

OZ   Postal headquarters in Washington
WIZARD   Postmaster General
BRIBE   Pension
DRAGGED THE BAG   Late delivery
LOCKER   Postal substation
BABY KILLERS   Overnight delivery services
DRIVE-BY   Postal employee on a murderous rampage
HORSE   Letter carrier
ABSENT WITHOUT LETTERS (AWOL)   Postal employee caught sleeping on the job
PAYROLL   Stamps
STAMP COLLECTING   Employee theft

e.g.—*"Part of the* **PAYROLL**'s *missing. The* **KGB** *is looking for a* **STAMP COLLECTOR**."*

NUT NOTE   Letter to Dear Abby
NO CLASS   First class
TURTLE TROLLEY   Overnight mail
POCKETBOOK   Mail bag
SHAKE 'N' FAKE   Medical leave

LAST CLASS   Second class
THINGS WITH WINGS   Airmail
FONDLED   Opened mail
GUNS 'N' BUNS   Illegal firearms and obscene materials

e.g.—*"There's going to be a lot of FONDLED mail around here if they're looking for GUNS 'N' BUNS."*

HICKS IN THE STICKS   Rural route
DONGHEADS   Congress

Prison Guard

SWING WING   Death row
CHESTER THE MOLESTER   Child rapist

e.g.—*"We just got a call from the SWING WING. They've got room for CHESTER THE MOLESTER now."*

DRAWER   Cell
BUREAU   Cellblock
SCREWDRIVER   Warden
CON TOUR   Inspection
IMMIGRANTS   Visitors; a.k.a. ALIENS
PROBE THE ROBE   Strip search
BIC HEAD   Arsonist
LARGE CHARGE   To hit with a stun gun

e.g.—*"We're gonna have to PROBE THE ROBE on that BIC HEAD. If he resists, give him a LARGE CHARGE."*

FILE   Bunk
FRENCH CUFF   White-collar criminal
STRIPPER RIPPER   Prostitute murderer
SOLE HOLE   Solitary confinement
BRAWL BALL   Riot
DON CON   Mafia convict
SLAM DUNK   Parole rejection

DICK-UP STICKUP   Armed rapist

e.g.—*"The parole board just SLAM DUNKED that DICK-UP STICKUP."*

RUSTY THE TRUSTY   Minimum security inmate
ROAD TOADS   Work detail; a.k.a. PEBBLE PUSHER, ROCK SOCKER
STIR-FRY   Electrocute; a.k.a. COOK THE CROOK
SHOCK-IT ROCKET   Electric chair
DOUBLE DIPPER   Multiple murderer
CLYDE   Armed robber

e.g.—*"Looks like they're gonna STIR-FRY that DOUBLE DIPPER tonight. I saw them checking the SHOCK-IT ROCKET."*

CRIME LINE   Record
LOUSE HOUSE   Prison
PEN PALS   Inmates
LOUISVILLE   Night stick
CRADLE SHOPPER   New prisoner
STOOL POOL   Protective custody
OPEN DOOR   Minimum security

e.g.—*"That CRADLE SHOPPER was a FRENCH CUFF. After he gets out of the STOOL POOL, he goes to the OPEN DOOR."*

THREW 'N' SCREW   Conjugal visit
RERUN   Repeat offender
JEWELRY   Hand and leg irons
STEEP SLEEP   Gas chamber

e.g.—*"Make sure you keep his JEWELRY on until you get him into the STEEP SLEEP."*

SWING DING   Execution by hanging
DOPE WITH THE ROPE   Executioner
TICKET PUNCHED   Pardoned
NO-GO SHOW   Parole hearing
KILL MILL   Execution chamber
HOT SHOT   Lethal injection
VACATE THE GATE   Attempted escape
OVERTIME   Extended sentence because of additional crimes

GIRDLE   Smuggle
DRUGS FOR THUGS (DFT)   Contraband
DOWN FOR THE COUNT   To receive a life sentence

e.g.—*"When the ALIEN tried to GIRDLE the DFT, we grabbed him."*

BOOKS FOR CROOKS (BFC)   Library
LIFT 'N' SIFT   Shakedown
BROOM ROOM   Prison industry shop
110 COMMANDMENTS   Rules and regulations

e.g.—*"I just checked the 110 COMMANDMENTS and found that RERUN has definitely got OVERTIME."*

LAST REPAST   Final meal
JAIL PAIL   Toilet
NAB 'N' GRAB   Confiscate
BLOCK THE SHOCK   Reprieve
SHIRK THE WORK   Strike
WHISPER   Informant
DERAIL THE MAIL   Open and read letters
FENCE DANCER   Escapee
CELLS WITH BELLS   Maximum security wing
CROC   Old con
BUTCHER SHOP   Exercise area
STOP THE DROP   Clemency and commutation of sentence
DRILL TEAM   Firing squad

e.g.—*"Damn! That SCREWDRIVER just STOPPED THE DROP. Go call the DRILL TEAM."*

YANKED 'N' SPANKED   Disciplined at an administrative hearing
BEARS ON THE STAIRS   Guard tier
SKEET RANGE   Watchtower
BLACKHEAD   Prisoner in administrative segregation

Private Investigator

SPADE Private investigator

LOOK 'N' SEE AT DMV Conduct a motor vehicle license and registration check

BACK DOOR To follow someone

HUMP DUMP Cheap motel

DISGUISED THE EYES Installed a camouflage camera

KODAK MOMENT Compromising photographs

PAPER TRAINED Bonded by an insurance company

*e.g.—"Check it out. I don't think that **SPADE**'s been **PAPER TRAINED**."*

MUDSLIDE Divorce case

SKID THE LID Sift and inspect garbage

PUT AN EARRING ON Place a phone tap

SHOCK TALK Threatening phone calls

RUM SHOE Alcoholic detective

SLUM SHOE Detective specializing in repossessions

FOOTPRINT Birth certificate

FLOUNDER Nonpaying debtor

BUSH PATROL Stakeout

SECOND SHIFT Adultery

*e.g.—"She thinks he's goin' on **SECOND SHIFT** now. We better get the **BUSH PATROL** out to the **HUMP DUMP**."*

TICKLE THAT TUMBLER Pick a lock

DROPOUT Missing person

PESTER LESTER Question neighbors

WHIFF Lead

BUG THE RUG Install tape recording equipment

HEARING AID Listening post

TED WASN'T DEAD Phony death claim

STAB AT THE TAB Do a credit check

BLOODHOUND Collection agency

OVERCHARGE THE CHARGE   Credit-card fraud
STOLE THE ROLE   Assumed the identity of another
NAME GAME   Use an alias
TRACK ASS   Look for hidden assets
GREYHOUND   Runaway
NEW LOAN   Embezzlement
FIRE SALE   Arson for profit

e.g.—*"They're blaming the FIRE SALE and the NEW LOAN on that GREYHOUND. If we're going to find him quick, we'll have to PESTER LESTER."*

MASK THE ASK   Make a discreet inquiry
DRAGGIN THE WAGON   Automobile repossession
HUNCHBACK   Married man or woman
MINUS LINUS   Missing heir (male)
EVE LEAVE   Missing heir (female)
WITLESS   Witness
PACKED A LUNCH   Left town
SLANT ON THE PLANT   Industrial security problem
WATCH THE SCOTCH   Suspected employee liquor theft
LOOK FOR THE CROOKS   Perform an activities check
CANNED THE HAND   Fired an employee
LEECH SHEET   Credit report
COKE QUIZ   Drug test; a.k.a. CRACK QUIZ
HIS STORY   Background investigation (male)
HER STORY   Background investigation (female)
SPACE TRACE   On-line computer search
BOND'S GONE   Bail jumper
FAX ATTACK   Facsimile interception

e.g.—*"He says the BOND'S GONE. You better do a SPACE TRACE and a FAX ATTACK right away."*

MUCK TRUCK   Surveillance van
LOBBY BOBBY   Hotel detective

e.g.—*"Call the LOBBY BOBBY and tell him we're gonna park the MUCK TRUCK near the service entrance."*

DUMB SHOE   Very stupid detective; a.k.a. NUMB SHOE
JAIL TRAIL   Prison record
CHIPPED   Beaten up
IRONCLAD GONADS   Tough guy

Psychiatrist

SEMISICK DICK (SSD)   Hypochondriac
BANANA SPLIT   Bipolar disorder
HEADBANGER   Psychiatrist
SHAKE, RATTLE, & ROLL   Electroshock treatment

e.g.—*"His former **HEADBANGER** says he's a **SEMISICK DICK**. I think he's a **BANANA SPLIT** who needs to **SHAKE, RATTLE, & ROLL**."*

CHEAP SLEEP   Hypnotherapy
CATNAPPER   Catatonic
SLO MO   Valium
FURNITURE MOVER   Hysterical patient; a.k.a. PLATE THROWER
ROLLER COASTER   Manic depressive
OUT TO LUNCH BUNCH   Group therapy
DOUBLE HEADER   Schizophrenic
SKINNY MINNIE   Anorexic
HURLER   Bulimic
NERO   Pyromaniac
SHRINK CLINK   Prison forensic unit
TRIPLE THREAT   Multiple personality
BATES MOTEL   Mental hospital

e.g.—*"According to the chart, the **TRIPLE THREAT** just checked out of the **BATES MOTEL**."*

RAIN MAN   Bedwetter
NIGHT FLIER   Sleepwalker; a.k.a. SLEEP CREEP
BRAIN TRAIN   Psychiatry internship
DEEP POCKET   Patient
MARTIAN   Insane patient

MOOD FOOD Halcion
CLEAVER FEVER Sociopathic personality
DRUG SLUG Substance abuser
FUCKED UP BAD (FUB) Demented

e.g.—*"Keep an eye on that **DRUG SLUG**. He's definitely a **FUB**. One of these days he'll get **CLEAVER FEVER**."*

HOP 'N' SKIPPER Euphoric
CANVAS COAT Straitjacket
TRENCH COAT Exhibitionist
SLEEPLESS SICKNESS Insomniac
FRIGHT RITE Phobia
NIXON Patient with a persecution complex
GRUNTER Primal therapy patient
TOPSPIN Vertigo
SLIDER Thorazine

e.g.—*"The **GRUNTER**'s complaining of severe **TOPSPIN**. Time to give him a **SLIDER**."*

HEAD SHED Couch
WEIRD BEARD Sigmund Freud
MIRROR Narcissist
THROW-UP Feedback
PANTS WAVER Nymphomaniac
PUNCH 'N' JUDY Role-playing
BLOT PLOT Rorschach test
GABBY ABBY Especially loquacious female patient
LIGHT FLIGHT Seasonal affective disorder
THREW Referral
WEAK SISTER Psychologist
WANDERER Patient with attention deficit disorder

e.g.—*"That **WEAK SISTER** just **THREW** me a **WANDERER**."*

LIZZIE BORDEN Split personality
PEARL HARBOR Panic attack
TWO-HANDER Behavior modification

e.g.—*"As soon as **LIZZIE BORDEN** was released from the **BATES MOTEL**, she **PEARL HARBORED**. She's a candidate for a **TWO-HANDER**."*

WET DREAM   Patient with multiple problems
LIFE RAFT   Codependent personality
HANDY ANDY   Kleptomaniac (male)
HANDY ANNIE   Kleptomaniac (female)
FLOP 'N' DROPPER   Narcoleptic
TAMMY   Patient with a severe character disorder
GROUNDER   Suicide by jumping
DRILL THE PILLS   Suicide by drug overdose
SMOG HOG   Suicide by carbon monoxide poison
STATUE   Autistic patient

e.g.—*"The newspaper didn't say whether that **STATUE** was a **GROUNDER** or a **SMOG HOG?**"*

SEEK 'N' PEEK   Voyeur
LOW TIDE   Depression
MIDGET'S NIGHTMARE   Inferiority complex
DONG NOT LONG   Impotence

e.g.—*"**DONG NOT LONG** is part of that **MIDGET'S NIGHTMARE**."*

BOOBY TRAP   Defense mechanism
BLEW UP   Had a nervous breakdown
FORTIES FEVER   Midlife crisis
HIP TO THE WHIP   Sadist
LONG FOR THE DONG   Person with penis envy; a.k.a. HANKER FOR A CRANKER, OGLE THE TOGGLE

e.g.—*"That **HANKER FOR A CRANKER**'s definitely **HIP TO THE WHIP**."*

MANIC PANIC   Paranoid; a.k.a. LUST FOR MISTRUST
JITTERS FOR CRITTERS   Patient unreasonably afraid of animals
STACKS OF JACKS   Multiple personality patient; a.k.a. GOBS OF BOBS
MOMMY NEAREST   Oedipus complex

Sex Therapist

COCK SOCK   Condom
CATCHER'S MITT   Diaphragm
BALLOON IN BLOOM   Unwanted pregnancy
WARMING UP   Foreplay
DICK STICK   Vibrator
ICEBOX   Frigid
BEAVER FEVER   Nymphomania
RELIEF PITCHER   Sexual surrogate

e.g.—*"Marilyn's problem is that she's either full of **BEAVER FEVER** or she's an **ICEBOX**. Maybe we need to get a **RELIEF PITCHER** in here."*

INVERT THE SKIRT   Female flirt
POGO STICK   Casanova
FINGER IN THE DYKE   Lesbian sex
BELLE OF THE BALL   Madam
SACRIFICE FLY   Premature ejaculation
REBUILT ENGINE   Penile implant
KNOCKER SOCCER   Fondle the breast
COCK POX   Venereal disease
CAP IT 'N' WRAP IT   Safe sex
DERRICK   Erection
THICK STICK   Large penis
TOMB IN THE WOMB   Barren
BLANK SPERM BANK   Sterile
CRACK JACK   Sperm donor
SHOOT TO FILL   In vitro fertilization
SLEEPING BEAUTY   Impotent client
BOX THAT TALKS   Especially talkative client
APPLIANCE DEPARTMENT   Sexual toys
TRICK DICK   Dildo

e.g.—*"**BOX THAT TALKS** wants to know what to do about **SLEEPING***

*BEAUTY. Maybe we should send her to the **APPLIANCE DEPARTMENT** to pick up a **TRICK DICK**."*

NICK THE DICK   Vasectomy
COCKEYED   Sexually promiscuous male
NO-HITTER   Virgin
PECKER WRECKER   Interrupted sex
TRIPLE HEADER   Ménage à trois
MATTRESS   Mistress
DIDDLE RIDDLE   Sexual problem
DRAGSTER   Cross dresser
TORQUE THE PORK   Sexual teasing
SALAMI SALESMAN   Male prostitute
HIT ONE OUT   Have an orgasm
TINY TATER   Small penis
SPLIT SHIFTER   Bisexual
THUMP THE HUMP   Sexual masochism

e.g.—*"We've definitely got a **DIDDLE RIDDLE** here. The wife likes to **TORQUE THE PORK** with a **SALAMI SALESMAN**, claiming her husband's only good for a **SACRIFICE FLY** and can never **HIT ONE OUT**. The husband's problem is that he's a **SPLIT SHIFTER** who likes to **THUMP THE HUMP**."*

HEN   Egg donor
MATE DATE   Husband/wife swapper; a.k.a. MATE BAIT
BASE ON BALLS   One-night stand
BALL MAUL   Man-hater
DONG WRONG   Inappropriate sex partner
MEATWAGON   Sexually promiscuous woman
BOX SCORE   Sexual therapy advice
SCREEN DOOR   Sexually uninhibited
CHEEK SPEAK   Phone sex
BIG HIT   Sexual intercourse
FASTBALL   Hurried sexual relations
STRIKE HIM OUT   Reject sexual advances
SEVEN ON THE RICHTER SCALE   Extremely intense orgasm

e.g.—*"According to her, she reached SEVEN ON THE RICHTER SCALE only with that BASE ON BALLS."*

SHADE MAID   Voyeur
SCORN THE PORN   Disinterested in erotica
PREMEDITATED MURDER SPREE   PMS
LIP STICK   Fellatio
BOX LUNCH   Cunnilingus
HOG-TIED   Bondage
CREW-CUT FRIEND   Lesbian

e.g.—*"Those two fight about everything: LIP STICK, BOX LUNCH, DICK STICKS, SACRIFICE FLIES, you name it. She says that he's a COCKEYED SHADE MAID. He says that although she SCORNS THE PORN, she's a SPLIT-SHIFTING BALL MAUL who wants to be HOG-TIED by her CREW-CUT FRIEND."*

SLIP A LOG IN THE DOG   Bestiality
HUMP SLUMP   Diminished sexual interest
SLAM JAM   Lubricant
SADDLE TRAMP   Prostitute
BALLS THEM ALL   Group sex with several men
BEANBALL   Sadist

Stewardess

MOE   Pilot
LARRY   Copilot
CURLY   Navigator
DUNGEON   Cockpit
HITCHHIKER   Someone without a ticket
TOE TAG   Boarding pass
NO CLASS   First class

e.g.—*"If he doesn't have a TOE TAG, throw the HITCHHIKER out. I'll go see if MOE, LARRY, and CURLY have made it to the DUNGEON yet."*

CLOSET HOPPER   Male steward

HOUSE Fat passenger
FLAMETHROWER Seat

e.g.—*"Watch that CLOSET HOPPER try and get the HOUSE into the FLAMETHROWER."*

ANTS Maintenance crew
BINGO Major air crash; a.k.a. UNSCHEDULED LANDING (UL)
EJECT Take off

e.g.—*"Tell those ANTS to check out the fan intake again. I don't wanna have a BINGO when we EJECT."*

FRENCH KISS Midair collision
WHITE HAIR O'Hare Airport
MANSON Air-traffic controller; a.k.a. ATC (alcohol, tobacco, and cocaine addict)
PARK THE CAR Assigned altitude and heading by the air-traffic controller
LOST HIS KEYS Controller who fails to keep track of his planes

e.g.—*"Hear about that FRENCH KISS at WHITE HAIR yesterday? The MANSON musta forgot where he PARKED THE CAR."*

SPUTTER 'N' STUTTER Stall
BROKE A SPOKE Engine failure
CLAW First-time flyer
ETNA Smoker
POKER Button-pusher
TENPINS Unattended children
SLOP SHOP Galley
FAUCET Nervous flyer; a.k.a. SWEATER
SHARK BAIT Life jacket

e.g.—*"This is gonna be a fun flight. I've spotted two CLAWS, an ETNA, and a POKER. There are a couple of TENPINS in the SLOP SHOP already and the FAUCET keeps playing with her SHARK BAIT."*

LOST THE DEFROST Deicer malfunction
BISECTOR Seat belt
SNORT Oxygen
DOA Dead on airplane

BOOT CHUTE   Emergency exit
KITE ENGINEER   Flight engineer
MARX BROTHERS   Control tower
KAMIKAZE   Japanese passenger
FART   Wind shear
FULL TRAY   Overcrowded airplane
R.O.O.F.   Run out of fuel
PRAYER BREAKFAST   Close call; a.k.a. NEW UNDIES
STALLING   Circling the airport waiting to land

e.g.—*"Call the **MARX BROTHERS**. Tell 'em there's lots of **FARTS** up here and if we have to keep **STALLING** with a **FULL TRAY** of **KAMIKAZES**, we're gonna **R.O.O.F.** We've had one **PRAYER BREAKFAST** already."*

COMA   Automatic pilot
FIDEL   Hijacker
CONNECT THE DOTS   Flight plan
FINGER   Gun
CANNOLI   Italian passenger

e.g.—*"Tell **MOE** to put it in a **COMA** and get back here. I've got a **FIDEL** who wants to see the **CONNECT THE DOTS**. He's got a **FINGER** on a **CANNOLI**."*

EARACHE   Talkative passenger; a.k.a. SHARPTON
YUGO   Small commuter plane; a.k.a. LIGHTER, DROP FLY, TREETOP
HOP 'N' DROP   Bad weather
DENSE AT THE FENCE   Many planes being held at the gate
SACK   Uniform
STUKA   German passenger
BULLET HOLE   Indian passenger
LIGHT SHOW   Electrical storm

e.g.—*"I hope we run into a **LIGHT SHOW** soon. **STUKA** and **BULLET HOLE** keep grabbing my **SACK**."*

ROACH RATS   Coach passengers
CAR BOMB   Irish passenger; a.k.a. GOTH
BODY BAG   Suitcase
DROP SHOP   Rest room

NO HANDS Instrument flying
TOOTHPASTE Severe injuries caused by a sudden violent depressurization
BUMPER Clumsy passenger
CRASHBAIT Frequent traveler
CLOSET Overhead storage bin

e.g.—*"That **BUMPER** can't be **CRASHBAIT**, can he? He keeps hitting himself with the **CLOSET** door."*

BLOW SHOW Air sickness
TRIM THE TREES Take off
GAG BAG Air sickness bag
STY IN THE EYE Poor visibility
CRASH PATCH Runway

Stockbroker

DESPERATE JUMP IN THE ALLEY (DJA) Dow Jones Average
SOAKER Broker
SHOOT TO KILL (STK) Hostile takeover
SNEAKY EVIL CRETINS Securities and Exchange Commission
LICORICE Commission
DOW BOY Speculator
WALK THE PLANK Forced sell-off
HOSTAGE TAKING Profit taking
HEMLOCK STOCK Pharmaceutical securities

e.g.—*"I just talked to a **DOW BOY**; he's convinced that after that **HOSTAGE TAKING**, they're gonna have to **WALK THE PLANK** with that **HEMLOCK STOCK**."*

FLEA MARKET Commodities exchange
RIDIN 'N' SLIDIN Slump
HOLDUP ARTIST Holding company head
BULLSHITISH Bullish
INSECURITIES Securities
STOCKS IN HOCK Securities purchased on margin

LOWBROW Common stock
FREE-FALL Stock market crash
SCRAP Junk bonds
DENTURES Debentures
CAPTAIN BID Corporate raider
FLOCK Block
BULL CHIP Blue chip
LAPTOP LAPDOG Declining computer stocks
LOAD O' SODA Lots of beverage stocks

e.g.—*"The **LAPTOP LAPDOGS** have been low for a while. I'm gonna buy a **LOAD O' SODA** instead."*

MILKMAN Michael Milken
LEDGE LEAPER Panic
DIRECTION ERECTION Rally
SCREAM SCREEN Big Board; a.k.a. SCAM SCAN

e.g.—*"I can't figure it out; either we're getting a **LEDGE LEAPER** or a **DIRECTION ERECTION**. How do you read the **SCREAM SCREEN?**"*

PIT BULL Commodity pit trader
FUTILES Future public utility offerings
WAL-MART Discount broker
SHOCK MARKET Stock market
TROJAN WHORES Inside traders
AMOEBA Stock split
CRASH OR CASH Buyout
BORED WITH FORDS Down on auto stocks
GARBAGE MAN Arbitrager
OVERTHREW THE CREW Corporate takeover
STAPLER Office supply manufacturing company
STREET WALKER Acquisition specialist
SHOCK CLOCK Stock ticker
WHIPS 'N' CHAINS Stocks and bonds
REAR ENTRY Take a company private; a.k.a. DROP SEAT
SCREWED Merged
MILKEN Churn stock to generate a commission
SATCHEL Portfolio

e.g.—*"He keeps that **SATCHEL MILKENED** for lots of **LICORICE**."*

RASH   Dividend
BABY   New stock
COLICKY BABY   Problematic new stock issue
ON THE HOOD   Over the counter
UNLOAD THE VIRGIN   Sell a new stock
BUMP   Correction
GRIZZLY   Bear market
STREETLIGHT   Investment banker who's taking a company public

e.g.—*"That **STREETLIGHT** thinks if we have a **BUMP** it's gonna be a **GRIZZLY**."*

007   Bond
BLITZKRIEG   Hostile takeover
BRAHMA   Bull market
SMASH FOR CASH   Break-up value of a company
TRAITOR   Trader
POLO PONY   Preferred stock
ARMPIT   Commodities trading area
ZORRO SAYS "BORROW"   Advisor who recommends margin purchases

Summer Camp Counselor

HOOF 'N' MOUTH   Camp physical
TOKEN   Poor kid
DOLT ON THE COLT   Poor horseback rider
LIFER   Full-season camper
BRICK   Athletically inept camper
TRIP SLIP   Application
GROUNDED OUT   Fell off the trampoline

e.g.—*"You mean he **GROUNDED OUT** again? Go check that **BRICK**'s **TRIP SLIP**. I sure hope he's not a **LIFER**."*

DEAD ANIMAL   Laundry bag

SHACK RACK   Bunk

e.g.—*"I couldn't find that **DEAD ANIMAL** until I looked under his **SHACK RACK**."*

FLEE TIME   Free time
HORSESHIT   Horseshoes; a.k.a. WHORE'S SHOES
GROUNDHOGS   Campers
GAS PASS   Meal ticket
AIRBAG   Obese camper

e.g.—*"That **AIRBAG** lost his **GAS PASS**. Go help him find it."*

LAST GASP   Asthmatic camper
TURNING BLUE SHOT   Flu vaccination
WANTED POSTER   Model camper
BAD DAD   Father
MOM BOMB   Mother
DRAGGIN THE LAKE   Looking for a lost camper
BALK AT THE WALK   Refuse to go on the hike
CRANE   Tall camper
LEAKING LENNY   Bedwetter (male)
SPURTING SALLY   Bedwetter (female)
SMELL HELL   Dining hall
MINI VINNY   Short camper; a.k.a. SMALL PAUL
DROP IT 'N' POP IT   Kitchen duty; a.k.a. BRING IT, DON'T FLING IT
FLOAT COAT   Life jacket
WATER BED   Drowning victim
BOX WITH SOCKS   Package or mail from home
CRYIN BRIAN   Homesick camper

e.g.—*"**CRYIN BRIAN**'s looking for a **BOX WITH SOCKS**."*

FRENCH FRIES   Black flies
DRESS THE BODY   Make the bed
BLAZER   Rich camper

e.g.—*"You better go talk to that **BLAZER**. He's refused to **DRESS THE BODY**."*

PART-TIMER   Two-week camper

PENCIL Skinny camper
ARROWHEAD Archery instructor
BROKEN NECK Diving instructor
COMMANDANT KLINK Camp director
SWAMP Camp kitchen

e.g.—*"ARROWHEAD and BROKEN NECK are supposed to meet COMMANDANT KLINK in the SWAMP."*

HOLLER BOX Public address system
JOHN PATROL Latrine duty
NOSEBLEED Socially unskilled camper
THREE ALARMER Bonfire
GERM LINER Contagious camper
SICK SHIP Infirmary
CARTS OF TRASH Arts and crafts
CATCH THE SCRATCH Become infected with poison ivy
FIELD OF SCREAMS Woodland filled with poisonous shrubs and plants

e.g.—*"Tell 'em they're going to CATCH THE SCRATCH if they get near the FIELD OF SCREAMS."*

TOW 'N' THROW Water ski; a.k.a. SNAG 'N' DRAG
CHERRY FERRY Motor boat
CRUMB SLUM Cabin
CLAMP THE LAMP Turn the lights out; a.k.a. BREAK THE BULB
CRACKED A HEEL DAY Track and field day
REEKING BAG Sleeping bag

e.g.—*"First get in your REEKING BAG and then BREAK THE BULB."*

STORE THE GORE Clean up
SKUNKS IN THE BUNKS Cabin inspection

Telephone Operator

SPIN IT AGAIN Redial

DORK NAMED BORK (DNB) Wrong number

e.g.—*"He got a **DORK NAMED BORK**. I told him to **SPIN IT AGAIN**."*

PAY OR DIE (POD) Collect call

BUTLER Answering machine

BOOM IT Hang up

MISPRINT Sprint

MIGHTY CRUMMY INSTALLATION MCI

EARTH TO MARS Long-distance call

EARS Phone tap

TURN 'N' BURN Reverse the charges

DECAYED PHONE Pay phone

CRAZY DAISY Crank caller; a.k.a. WACKY JACKY

STALL THE CALL Try to keep someone on the line long enough to trace it

e.g.—*"See if you can **STALL THE CALL** from this **WACKY JACKY**."*

MOAN BILL Monthly statement; a.k.a. GROAN BILL

STUPORVISOR Supervisor; a.k.a. STUPID LIAR

KREMLIN Business office

HANGNAIL Complaining customer

NERVOUS DEPARTMENT Service department

DROPPED A TABLE ON THE CABLE Severed an underground wire

ALONE ON THE PHONE Waiting for someone to come back on the line

e.g.—*"No wonder she's **ALONE ON THE PHONE**. It looks like someone **DROPPED A TABLE ON THE CABLE**. Call the **NERVOUS DEPARTMENT**."*

FLOPERATOR Operator

ATTILA AT&T

SHERMAN TO HERMAN Person-to-person call; a.k.a. CANDY TO SANDY

JUNGLE DRUM Overseas call

PHONY EXPRESS   Call forwarding
ZONE'S THE PHONE   A phone's area code
DESPAIR SERVICE   Repair service
SMALL CALL   Local number
DOLLAR CALLER   Toll call
SWEET SHEET   Rate schedule

e.g.—*"I can't tell from that **SWEET SHEET** if this is a **SMALL CALL** or a **DOLLAR CALLER**."*

MUTTER BOX   Telephone
STEEL WHEEL   Rotary phone
POLE TROLL   Lineman

e.g.—*"Get me the **NERVOUS DEPARTMENT**. That **POLE TROLL** needs a **STEEL WHEEL** and a **MUTTER BOX**."*

FREE PASS   800 number
SEVER THE LEVER   Disconnected
MISINFORMATION   Information
CALL GIRL   Account representative
WELT ON THE BELT   Beeper
POP BOX   Push-button phone
PHONE ON THE THRONE   Telephone installation
CLICK STICK   Telephone pole
BLOWN PHONES   Dead lines
LOP THE LINE   Hang up
THROBBIN ROBIN   Obscene phone caller
WHIR 'N' PURR   Dial tone
CON JOB   Conference call
MISSED THE LIST   Unpublished phone number
GAB TAB   Service fee
STATIC IN THE ATTIC   Bad connection
FLOWN BOOK   Phone book
COLD HOLD   Call-waiting device
SNAKE   Switchboard
LIMBO   Hold

e.g.—*"He's getting pretty upset. The **SNAKE**'s got him in **LIMBO**."*

NO TONE ON THE PHONE   Problem line
JUICED THE BOOTH   Vandalized the booth

e.g.—*"I'm gonna call the **DESPAIR SERVICE**. They've got **NO TONE ON THE PHONE**. Maybe somebody **JUICED THE BOOTH**."*

DIZZY SIGNAL   Busy signal
AUTO BOX   Car phone
RECEIVER'S GOT A FEVER   Phone off the hook

e.g.—*"I keep getting a **DIZZY SIGNAL** from that **AUTO BOX**. I think the **RECEIVER'S GOT A FEVER**."*

COCK TALK   Phone sex service
LOAN THE PHONE   Lease the equipment
CRACKS IN THE FAX   Facsimile machine in need of repair
CUSS SOME MORE   Customer
BUZZ SCUZZ   Static
EXPIRE ON THE WIRE   Caller dies because he can't reach a 911 number

Truck Stop Operator

FLYPAPER   Speed trap
WALLET WHOMPER   Speeding ticket
BUMPER HUMPER   Tailgater
ROSARY   Rotary
DEATH VALLEY   Steep downgrade; a.k.a. ROLLER COASTER
DEATH RAY   Radar
SUBWAY   Underpass
RALLY ALLEY   Passing lane
TROOPER SNOOPER   Radar detector
WALDO   Sheriff
BUDGE THE SLUDGE   Fix a frozen engine
DIESEL WEASEL   Mechanic
FATHEAD   Flatbed truck

e.g.—*"Have the **DIESEL WEASEL** go over and see if he can **BUDGE THE SLUDGE** on that **FATHEAD**."*

FROST HEAVE Refrigerated truck; a.k.a. CHILLY BILLY
STICK 'N' SPIT Check the oil and water
CRUSH HOUR Rush hour
DUNG HEAP Traffic jam
FULL DECK Multilevel interchange
BUN SLINGER Waitress
TRACK STAR Someone who didn't pay the bill
BUST Bus
FORK BRAIN Dishwasher
SAL MONELLA Short-order cook
BUMPER JUMPER Illegal immigrant
MEX DETECTS Immigration check point
PEDAL PUSHER Speeder
GOLD ROAD Toll road
CREAM CHEESE Chain reaction pileup
WINTERSTATE Snow-covered interstate
BANDIT Toll taker
PRETZEL Cloverleaf
WATER SLIDE Wet road
HANDSTAND Rollover
HUNGRY Empty truck

e.g.—*"I just saw **CHILLY BILLY** do a **HANDSTAND** on the **WATER SLIDE**. Lucky for him, he was **HUNGRY** at the time."*

DECEIT RECEIPT Altered manifest
COW SCOW Cattle truck
DUCK TRUCK Dangerous, uninspected rig; a.k.a. TRUCK AMOK
FLAMEOUT Stalled engine
QUEER GEAR Slipped clutch
DONUT Tire
GLAZED DONUT Recapped tire
SOFA Motor home
HISS LIST Menu
ZIPPERHEAD Biker

e.g.—*"Tell the **BUN SLINGER** that the **ZIPPERHEAD** wants a **HISS LIST**."*

MAKIN BACON   Piggyback trailer

FIX THE SHOES   Replace the brakes

THUMB SUCKERS   Tourists

MESSED ROOM   Rest room

THICK SLICK   Diesel gas

SPILL IT 'N' FILL IT   Oil change

PUBLIC JERK   Public works

WALKIE-TALKIE   Hitchhiker

WHITE FRIGHT   Snow storm

DEATH WISH   Motorcycle

RIG PIG   Prostitute

BLACKTOP COP (BTC)   State trooper

VIDIOT   Video game player

BACTERIA   Cafeteria

e.g.—*"Give this change to that **VIDIOT** while I see if the **FORK BRAIN** is in the **BACTERIA**."*

SCAB SLAB   Counter

TABLE IN THE STABLE   Booth

TAR CZAR   Highway patrol

SPEED 'N' WEED   Drugs for sale

VAN MAN   Truck driver

COP STOP   Road block

GRAB A CAB   Hijack a truck

SLEEP WITH THE SHEEP   Budget motel

Waiter

CHILD MOLESTER   Patron who doesn't tip

IGOR   Apprentice cook

FOSSILS   Diners who take a long time to eat; a.k.a. CAMPERS

STILL WALKING   Cooked rare

e.g.—*"Hey, **IGOR**! Make sure that prime rib's **STILL WALKING**. I've got a party of **FOSSILS** at table number 2 and a **CHILD MOLESTER** at table number 8."*

MILKEN   Someone who bolts without paying the bill; a.k.a. BOESKY
HACKER   Smoker
SWILL MILL   Buffet table

e.g.—*"Watch that HACKER by the SWILL MILL. I think he'll pull a MILKEN."*

PEON   Busboy
PIGPEN   Dining room
DUMP   Kitchen; a.k.a. PIT
ICU   Bar

e.g.—*"While I'm in the DUMP, have the PEON get those HACKERS outta the ICU and into the PIGPEN."*

WET DIAPER   Unruly child
CIGAR   Hot dog

e.g.—*"Throw that WET DIAPER a CIGAR, will ya?"*

GROG LOG   Wine list
K MART   Generic American beer
HIMMLER   Imported German beer
SPOON GOON   Dishwasher
PORK ON THE FORK   Dirty silverware
TUBA   Loud patron
FLATLINERS   People who try to make reservations in restaurants that don't take them
BREAD BOX   Cash register
HEAVE 'N' LEAVE   Vomit
WIDE CLYDE   Obese customer (male)
WINNIE BAGO   Obese customer (female)

e.g.—*"Here, you talk to these FLATLINERS. That TUBA near the BREAD BOX looks like he's gonna HEAVE AND LEAVE on WIDE CLYDE."*

SCARF 'N' BARF   Surf and turf
FLOATER   Catch of the day
BOWL BAIT   Appetizer
BOUNCED   Dropped food on the floor
ANN O'REXIA   Emaciated-looking person

WART   A particularly unattractive, slovenly diner

DINOSAUR   Elderly patron

CRACKER   Customer who eats a lot of munchies

BACKDOOR SPECIAL   Greasy, gassy food

CANCER WARD   Smoking section

BUSHMEN   Vegetarians

RECYCLE   To stretch the food supply and make other meals by using leftovers

SIX-PACK   Table for six

e.g.—*"I need a **SIX-PACK**. Send **CRACKER** and the **BUSHMEN** into the **CANCER WARD**. I'm going to the **PIT** to **RECYCLE** this **BACKDOOR SPECIAL**."*

SMASH THE HASH   Cook the food quickly

FROG GROG   French wine

PROM KING   Underaged drinker

MAGNET   Patron who tries to sponge food or drink off other customers

GROPIN   Illicit sex in a darkened restaurant booth

e.g.—*"The **PROM KING**'s **MAGNET** looks like she's hopin' for some **GROPIN**."*

LOCUSTS   People who eat food remnants off someone else's plate; a.k.a. ANTEATERS

HIROSHIMA   Microwave

LYNCHIN LUNCHEON   Fried chicken

BB   Back booth

e.g.—*"Time to **HIROSHIMA** that **LYNCHIN LUNCHEON** for those **LOCUSTS** in the **BB**."*

SICK DICK   Drunkard

SWINE FU   Chinese food

HUNS   Diners, especially children, with bad manners

PAYBACK   Food poisoning

e.g.—*"Tell the **SICK DICK** and the rest of his **HUNS** that if they don't like it here, they can waddle out the door and get some **SWINE FU** instead. Maybe we'll luck out and they'll get a dose of **PAYBACK**."*

JAP FRAPPE   Japanese food

PIG SICK   Trichinosis

CRO-MAGNONS   People who eat with their hands

CLOT   Any rich, fat-laden dessert

MONKEY CHOW   Indian food

e.g.—*"I've been watching those **CRO-MAGNONS** so long, I'm in the mood for some **MONKEY CHOW** or maybe just a **CLOT**."*

SOUP DUPE   Waiter

GAS 'N' DOGS   Beans and franks

STABLE TABLE   Booth for fat people